Past-into-Present Series

THE MIDLANDS

Clive Gilbert

B.T.BATSFORD LTD London

First published 1978

ISBN 0 7134 0497 3

Printed in Great Britain by
Cox & Wyman Ltd, Fakenham
for the Publishers B.T. Batsford Ltd
4 Fitzhardinge Street, London W1H 0AH

Acknowledgment

The Author and Publishers thank the following for their kind permission to reproduce copyright illustrations:

Aerofilms Ltd for figs 1, 2, 6, 13, 18 and 59; Birmingham Central Libraries for figs 23 and 25; Blake for figs 34, 37 and 61; Janet Bord for fig 7; the British Library Board for fig 8; Peter Clayton for fig 3; HM Stationery Office with the sanction of the Controller (Crown copyright reserved) for fig 57; Leicestershire County Council – Museums, Art Galleries and Records Service for figs 14 and 32; Longman Group Ltd (photograph A.N. Smith) for fig 29; the Mansell Collection for figs 15, 17, 26, 30, 31, 39 and 41; Montagu Motor Museum for fig 43; National Coal Board for fig 21; Nottinghamshire Record Office for fig 19; Popperfoto for fig 35; Radio Times Hulton Picture Library for figs 22, 24, 27, 28, 33, 34, 40, 42, 45, 50 and 51; Edwin Smith for figs 10 and 11; University of Reading Museum of English Rural Life for fig 19; Wedgwood Group for fig 16; John Whybrow Collection for figs 48, 49, 53 and 54.

Figures 4, 5, 9, 55, 56, 58 and 60 are based on information and illustrations in the following publications: fig 4 – Alan R.H. Baker and J.B. Harley (ed.), *Man Made the Land*, David and Charles; fig 5 – H.C. Darby (ed.), *A New Historical Geography of England*, Cambridge University Press; fig 9 – C.J. Bond, 'Deserted Medieval Villages in Warwickshire: a Review of Field Evidence', *Transactions of the Birmingham Archaeological Society*; figs 55, 56 and 58 – C.R. Gilbert, *Towns and Cities* (Wayland Regional Studies – the Midlands), Wayland; fig 60 – Ivor H. Seeley, *Outdoor Recreation and the Urban Environment*, Macmillan.

Figures 12, 44, 46, 47 and 52 are the property of the Author. Figure 40 is the property of the Publishers.

Contents

The Illustrations

1
The Making of the Midland Landscape

A longer time-span separates the first Roman invasion of Britain (55 B.C.) from the Norman Conquest (1066) than the period between the rule of Alfred the Great (871-99) and the landing of a man on the moon (1969). Yet the Norman armies that entered the Midlands after 1066 would have been confronted by a landscape that had changed little from that encountered by Roman legionnaires. Large herds of deer roamed undisturbed across Cannock Chase, wild boars crashed through the great forests that stretched from the Welsh borders to the Peak District, huge flocks of wading birds reared their young in the eastern wetlands and eagles soared over the Shropshire hills. Man, however, had made an indelible mark upon the land.

The story of Midland England up to 1086 is one of gradual colonization by successive waves of invaders. It is doubtful whether the population of the region exceeded 200,000 people by the time of the Domesday survey, yet many elements of the Midland landscape had been firmly established by that date. Almost every hamlet and village that we know today, apart from those that originated during the industrial revolution, had been founded before the end of the eleventh century. So too had hundreds of country churches and many thousands of miles of rural tracks and footpaths. Modern parish boundaries largely pre-date the Norman Conquest as do many sites of primitive industrial activity. The agricultural riches of areas like the Vale of Evesham had been exploited for many centuries prior to the Roman occupation and men fished the Severn for spawning salmon before the birth of Christ. Finally, commercial activity, based upon such towns as Worcester, Leicester, Nottingham and Northampton, had made its appearance by 1086.

The Midland landscape therefore, although a product of many centuries of varying economic, social and political forces, largely owes its character to a handful of immigrants who, through successive generations, tackled and shaped a wilderness.

Early Colonization

Forty years ago, the archaeologist Sir Cyril Fox described central England as 'the heavily wooded Midlands where pre-Roman occupation of any kind is likely to have been scanty or transient or both'. This statement has since been challenged by a series of discoveries which have thrown light on the early colonization of the Midlands.

A systematic air-survey of the Avon valley has revealed prehistoric features which are too faint to be noticed on the ground. Certain rectangular enclosures may be fields of Neolithic date, and dark rings are interpreted as hut sites, while thick, concentric circles appear to be the remains of ceremonial monuments of the Bronze Age. Similar work carried out in the Trent and Severn valleys suggests that a few favoured river terrace sites with easily worked soils have been continuously settled for at least 5,000 years.

The most obvious legacies of the prehistoric period are the hill forts, the majority of which date from the Iron Age, probably reflecting a period of rapid expansion and colonization in the region. Upland fortifications vary

1 The wild landscape that confronted the differing peoples who sought to make the Midlands their home (the River Wye in the Welsh border country).

2 Old Oswestry Iron Age hill fort. British tribes, originally driven out by the Romans, re-occupied the fort in the fifth century but were finally expelled by Saxon invaders following the Battle of Maserfelth in AD 641.

in both size and complexity. Old Oswestry covers 16.2 hectares (40 acres) and consists of three huge earthen banks surrounded by an enormous double compound, whereas the smallest of Northamptonshire's three forts, Hunsbury, is a modest site of 1.6 hectares (four acres) enclosed by a single ditch. Many so-called forts were no more than cattle pounds and were probably never permanently occupied. Others, however, show evidence of a long period of settlement. At Croft Ambrey in Herefordshire clusters of hut circles and the foundation post holes of larger communal buildings point to a village capable of supporting over 200 people.

Although hill forts are scattered throughout the Midlands, particularly in the Welsh Marches and along the Cotswold escarpment, little is known of the social and economic life of their inhabitants. Celtic society was probably made up of family groups which joined together only for purposes of warfare; wealth was measured in terms of numbers of cattle, so frequent rustling occurred. During the later Iron Age certain tribes appear to have formed larger political units. The Coritani, descendants of the warlike Belgae who had invaded southern and eastern England from Germany in the first century BC, controlled virtually the whole of the East Midlands prior to the Roman occupation.

The Celtic economy was localized and subsistent, but inter-regional contact did take place. Neolithic axe-makers trod the Portway along the crest of the Long Mynd in Shropshire while the Jurassic Way (running from the Bristol Avon to the Humber via Banbury and Northampton) was a footpath of great antiquity before its use by Bronze Age pottery traders.

The Roman Occupation

The successful Roman invasion of AD 43 was followed by many subsequent attempts to conquer Britain by force. Following the surrender of the southern British tribes, the invaders pushed northwards and established a Midland frontier zone which ran from the Bristol Channel via the rivers Severn, Avon and Trent to the Humber. A 48-kilometres (30 miles) wide belt of militarily occupied country was serviced by the Fosse Way, one of the great Roman roads that may still be followed from Exeter to Lincoln via Bath and Leicester.

It is probable that Roman ambitions were limited initially to the productive English lowlands. But if the Romans intended to discard the densely wooded Midlands and the mountains of Wales, they reckoned without Caractacus. Leading a strong force, the British chief crossed the frontier in AD 47. A counter-attack drove the Britons back into Wales, but the Romans were forced to extend their occupied territory across the Midlands and establish a new frontier at the River Severn. In order to supply the border garrisons a network of roads was constructed. Strategic highways, such as Watling Street (which cuts through the southern side of the Trent valley from its junction with the Fosse Way to Viriconium on the Severn) and Icknield Street (following a northerly course from Alcester through the heart of Birmingham to Wall in

3 Tombstone of a Roman soldier shown riding down a Briton.

Staffordshire and on to Derby), were finished by AD 50, but another century passed before the majority of minor Roman roads that criss-cross the Midlands were completed.

In its early stages the Roman occupation was unremittingly harsh. Each tribal group was forced to provide its local military post with a substantial proportion of its corn harvest; young Midlanders were pressed into service with the Roman army in Europe or were drafted into road-building gangs. Resentment caused by such practices triggered the bloody revolt of the Celtic tribes of southern England in AD 60. Although it failed, the rebellion did prompt the Romans to change their style of government.

After the appointment of Julius Agricola as governor of the province in AD 77, the occupying power sought the co-operation rather than the submission of British chiefs. The latter were encouraged to speak Latin, wear the toga and adopt the Roman practice of living in towns. Native rulers and nobles who were prepared to collaborate were granted a limited measure of independence.

Town and Country in Roman Times

There is little doubt that the Midlands was a second-rate growth area during the period of Roman occupation. Nevertheless, certain significant social and economic changes did take place within the region. Foremost amongst these was the growth of towns.

Permanent settlements of any size invariably developed from Roman forts sited along strategic routeways. Many of these communities, such as the string of military stations astride Watling Street, did not survive the evacuation of the legions to fight in the North after AD 78, whereas others, like Worcester, Gloucester and Alcester, were able to develop as civil settlements serving a local agricultural population.

Roman towns were usually built to a gridiron pattern, outlined by a masonry wall pierced by gated entrances. Streets were paved and often provided with footpaths. A public water-supply was sometimes laid on, water being either drawn from a nearby river through iron-jointed wooden pipes or conveyed in an open trench. Leicester, a provincial capital, boasted a complex of important buildings including the forum or administrative centre, a public bath-house complete with under-floor heating, and perhaps an amphitheatre.

Despite the growth of towns, the wealth of the region was in agriculture. The Romans introduced no revolutionary farming methods, apart from the two-handled scythe and the iron-bladed spade, but their presence alone promoted an expansion of cultivated land. Roman roads provided British farmers with improved communications and Roman towns and garrisons gave them new markets for their surplus produce. These developments were restricted to the fertile valleys of the Severn and the Avon and to the partially reclaimed fens of the East Midlands. Upland areas such as the Birmingham Plateau and Cannock

Chase remained in their natural wooded state, being used only for hunting and as a source of charcoal.

The typical Roman villa (a relatively large, sophisticated dwelling of brick surrounded by farm buildings and perhaps a small temple) was unknown in the Midlands north of the Cotswold escarpment. Aerial photography has revealed the existence of only five modest farmsteads in the Avon valley. Elsewhere within the region farming appears to have changed little from that practised in the late Iron Age.

Industrial development during the occupation was modest. Lead was mined from the Shropshire hills at Snailbeach and iron ore was won from the Forest of Dean. Many of the larger settlements manufactured iron implements, pottery and other domestic goods for local inhabitants. In the Hartshill district of east Warwickshire, however, a large complex of pottery kilns, capable of producing in excess of local requirements, suggests an industry based upon widespread distribution of its wares. Regional marketing of industrial products has been confirmed by the discovery at Gloucester of tiles made in the Kenilworth and Nuneaton areas.

Anglo-Saxon Invasion and Settlement

The network of villas, farmsteads, roads, garrison and market towns established during almost 400 years of Roman rule did not survive the coming of the English.

From the fourth century onwards, Angle and Saxon invaders from the lowlands of Northern Europe gradually pushed their way westwards across Britain. Avoiding the densely wooded high ground, Saxon adventurers followed the Midland river valleys, blazing a trail that was to be followed in later years by increasing numbers of settlers.

By the year 600 the Midlands contained four major Saxon tribal groups. The Hwicce farmed the Avon valley, while the Magonsaete settled in the region of the lower Severn; the Middle Angles colonized the Fenlands, while the Mierce penetrated the middle Trent and Tame valleys.

The Saxons were a farming people who lived in villages rarely numbering more than two dozen families. The community worked large 'open' fields divided into narrow family strips which were separated by deep furrows. Hay meadows and grazing lands were held in 'common', each villager sharing the right of usage. As the population of a village increased, surrounding woodland was further cleared for planting and grazing. Eventually distance from the village to the new fields became so great that a 'daughter settlement' was formed. Place names recall this process: in Worcestershire the villages of North, Middle and South Littleton suggest two offshoots from the original settlement,

4 The three-field system adopted through much of the Midlands by Saxon villagers.

while in a corner of east Warwickshire the name 'Whitacre' occurs in five separate villages.

Saxon settlement of the Midlands was responsible for more than just the village geography of the region. Parish and county boundaries date largely from the Saxon period: so too do the routes of many thousands of miles of country roads. The Saxons introduced the method of dating historical events from the birth of Christ, pounds-shillings-and-pence, coronations, a system of national taxation and, of course, the English language. But perhaps their greatest achievement was in changing for ever the look of the land. From the sixth century the great forests that cloaked the Midlands were gradually colonized. The 'natural' Midland countryside of scattered woodlands, irregular fields and winding hedgerows was man-made.

The Rise and Fall of Mercia

The Kingdom of Mercia was created by the military exploits of Penda, a minor member of the royal house of the Mierce. During the early seventh century the Mercians established their authority over the lesser Saxon tribes of the Midlands and drove the British westwards beyond the River Severn. Having secured its southern border by defeating the West Saxons of Wessex at Cirencester in 628, Mercia embarked on a struggle with Northumbria which was to continue for 90 years.

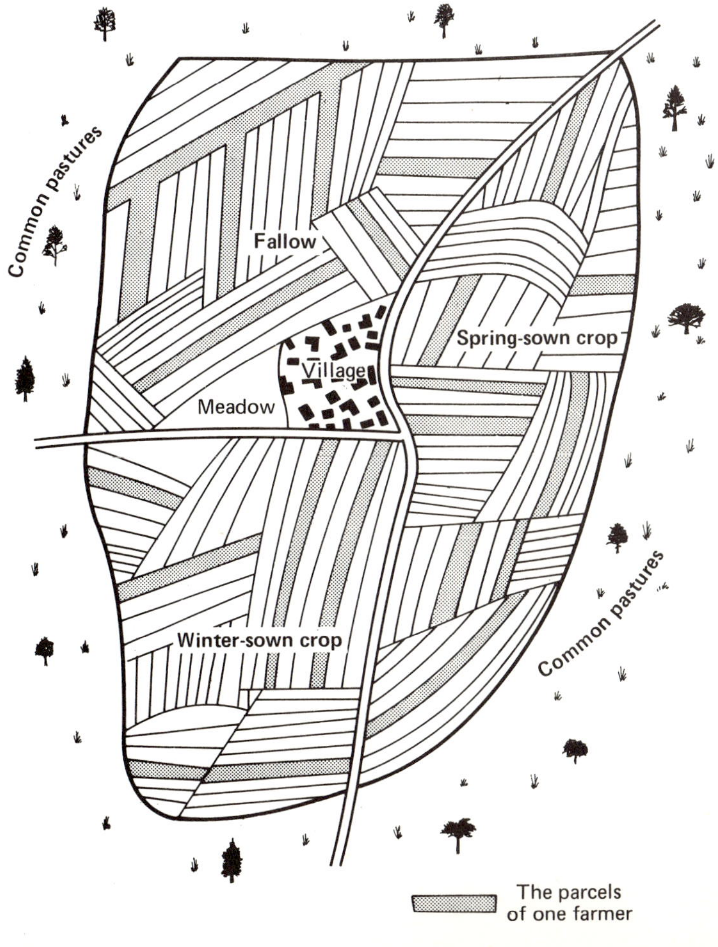

In his initial campaigns Penda scored a series of crushing victories over the Northumbrians, but in 654, having advanced as far as Bamburgh on the north-east coast, the Mercian forces were defeated and Penda himself was killed. This reversal of Mercian fortunes was not finally checked until the accession of Aethelbald in 716.

5 Political divisions about 800 AD, shortly after the death of Offa.

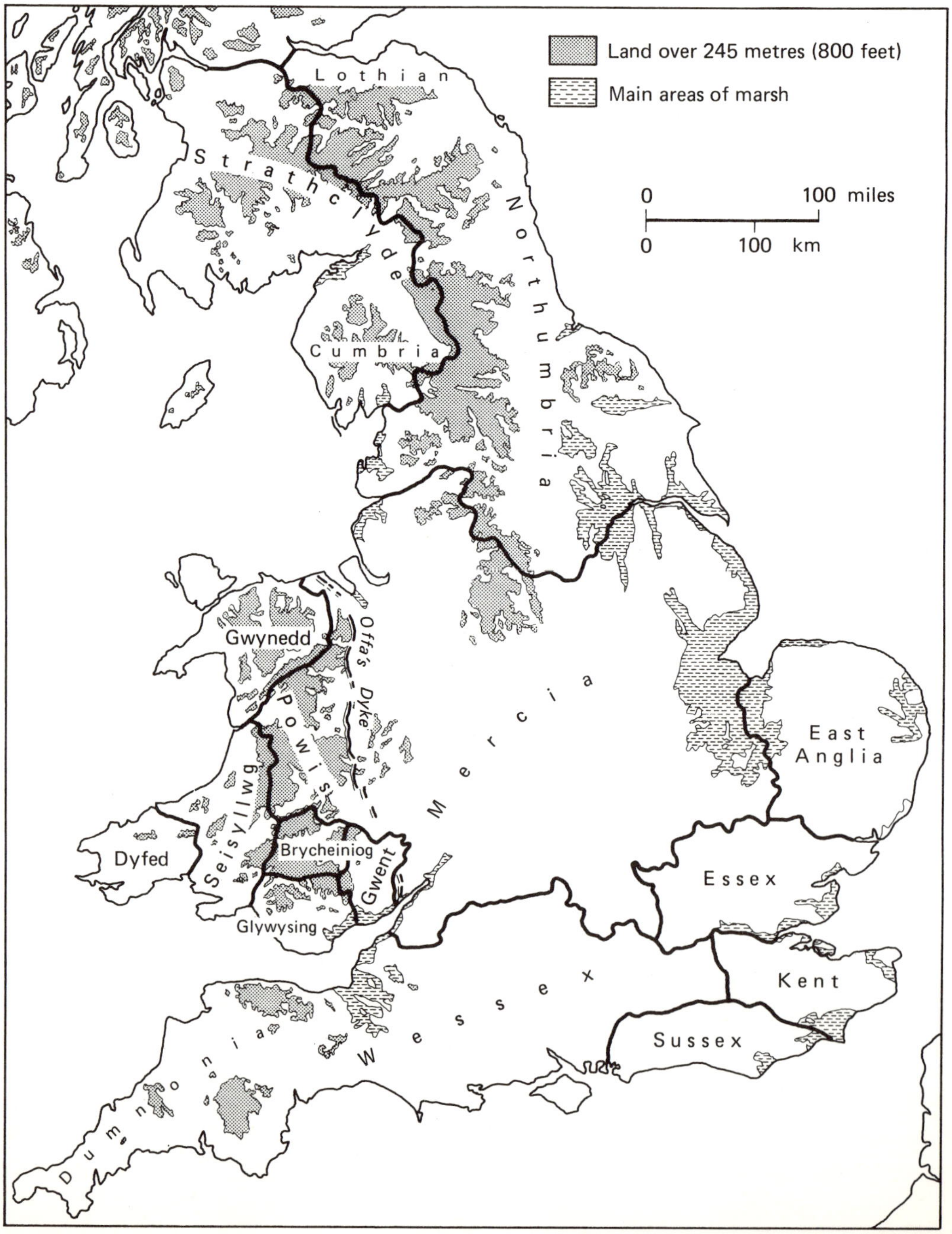

Throughout his reign Aethelbald concentrated not on the failing power of Northumbria but on the growing threat from the West Saxons. Conquest of modern Somerset and of the kingdoms of Kent and Essex provided bases for an assault upon the Wessex heartland, which culminated in a decisive Mercian victory in 755. Aethelbald, however, did not live to enjoy his triumph; two years later he was murdered and, while rival claimants fought for the Mercian crown, Wessex regained its former lands in southern England.

The Mercian civil war was decided in favour of Offa who, during his 35-year rule, extended the power of Mercia – either by conquest or diplomacy – throughout Saxon Britain. Yet Offa was more than just a warrior-king; he established a code of law, introduced a uniform coinage, encouraged trade with Europe and erected the first cathedral at Lichfield. His lasting monument is Offa's Dyke, a great earthwork built from the River Dee to the Bristol Channel to define the border between the Mercians and the Welsh. The Dyke reveals a degree of engineering skill and control of material resources far beyond the capabilities of any earlier English king.

Allegiance, though, was owed to the king and not to the kingdom. With Offa's death in 791 internal rebellions ripped Mercia apart. A further 40 years of fighting, chiefly against Egbert of Wessex, left the Mercians with little strength to meet a new enemy – Danish invaders who stormed across the East Midlands after 865. By 877 Mercia had been divided between the Danes, who colonized the region to the north of the River Welland, and the Saxons, ruled by Ceolwulf, a puppet of the invading hordes.

The Danes were eventually pushed north of the Humber in 918, by the forces of Edward of Wessex, but instead of regaining its independence Mercia was absorbed into the emerging English nation. A name, the foundations of Warwick and Tamworth castles, the ruined forts of Bridgnorth, Stafford and Eddisbury and the great Dyke in the west are all that remain of the first and last Midland kingdom.

Conquest and Control

The Anglo-Danish struggle for the crown of England was not resolved until the Norman Conquest of 1066 and the accession to the throne of Duke William of Normandy. Having won his prize, William was forced to defend it in the Roman manner – by military strength and firm government.

English resistance in the Midlands was sporadic and localized. A rebellion by Eric the Wild in Herefordshire in 1067 was put down with a massive show of force which left the countryside devastated. Similar treatment was handed out to those North Midland shires which gave assistance to an abortive uprising in 1070. In the words of a twelfth-century monk, William 'fell on the English like a ravening lion, commanded their houses and corn, with all their implements and chattels, to be burnt . . . and large herds of cattle and beasts of burden to be butchered wherever they were found'.

Savage reprisals were not William's only method of protecting his crown. By 1085 a chain of castles had been built across the Midlands. Some were simply mounds of earth and rock surmounted by a ditch while others, such as Warwick, Ludlow and Nottingham, were massive strongholds built of stone, capable of housing large detachments of soldiers and of withstanding a long siege.

In return for military support during the Conquest and for continuing assistance during the subjugation of the English, Norman nobles were installed in the new fortresses and rewarded with extensive tracts of land. Thus Hugh de Grentmesnil was entrusted with the defence of Leicester and given large estates throughout the East Midlands, from which he exacted payments of money, grain and livestock. The most senior and trustworthy of the Norman nobles, those related to William by blood, were placed in those areas most vulnerable to attack. Hence the Welsh Marches were divided into three powerful earldoms (Hereford, Shrewsbury and Chester) that protected the westward flow of Anglo-Norman colonization beyond Offa's Dyke.

By 1086 about one-fifth of all the land in England south of the River Tyne was held by the King, about one-quarter was in the hands of the Church and nearly one-half had been granted to the greater Norman barons. What the Romans could not do in 400 years, nor the Mercians in 300, William had accomplished in 20.

6 Ludlow Castle, a major link in the chain of fortresses built by the Normans to defend their territory against the Welsh.

The Domesday Inquest

The geographer, H.C. Darby, has referred to the Domesday Book as 'probably the most remarkable statistical document in the history of Europe'. The information recorded by William's investigators in 1086 paints a detailed picture of demographic and economic conditions in the Midland shires.

The population of England had risen from some 350,000 on the eve of the Roman invasion to about 1¾ million by 1086. Despite centuries of patient

7 Church porch, Kilpeck, Herefordshire. This magnificent Norman doorway dates from 1134 although a more ancient Saxon church once stood on the site.

clearing and planting by generations of Anglo-Saxon immigrants, the Midlands remained sparsely peopled. The Domesday survey reveals that the whole of Northamptonshire contained fewer people than modern Kettering, Leicestershire had about as many as modern Coalville and Nottinghamshire had only 20,000 people altogether. To the north and west population densities declined. Less than five persons per square mile inhabited Staffordshire and Derbyshire compared to some 10-15 persons in parts of Warwickshire and over 20 in prosperous districts of Norfolk and Sussex. Such low figures were not simply the result of an inhospitable environment, for the Conqueror's army had laid waste to wide tracts of land, destroying many villages. The Domesday entry for the town of Stafford records a total number of 179 houses, but 51 of these were deserted. Similar devastation is noted in Herefordshire and Shropshire, but this was partly caused by Welsh raiding.

Agricultural development had proceeded furthest in the fertile valley of the Avon and along the lower reaches of the Severn and Trent rivers. Brailes, now a small village astride the Warwickshire Stour, boasted 51 ploughteams, wide meadows for grazing and a watermill. Birmingham, on the other hand, could muster only three ploughteams.

The pattern of farming is reflected in the growth of towns during the eleventh century. Worcester, Pershore and Droitwich were important commerical centres by 1086, the latter deriving its considerable wealth from the salt trade. Warwick had grown around its castle to number over 200 properties, while the new borough of Nottingham included 48 merchants' houses. Setbacks did occur (Shrewsbury, for example, saw 51 of its houses ripped down for use in the construction of the castle) but the overall trend was one of steady expansion.

Industrial activity is rarely mentioned in the Domesday survey. Whether the paucity of information reflects accurately the situation in the eleventh century or a lack of interest by William's agents is not known. As the purpose of the Domesday Book was to make tax collection easier it is reasonable to suppose that returns from industrial working were grossly inferior to those of agriculture and were consequently ignored. Ironworks are recorded at Corby and Gretton in the ironstone belt of Northamptonshire, in the Forest of Dean and at Wilnecote in Warwickshire. Lead-working is entered for six places in the Derbyshire Peak District but the survey ignores the Shropshire Hills. Elsewhere the Book occasionally mentions smiths. At Dudley the smith seems to have been the only free man, indicating a position of some importance. There is no real evidence of an iron trade in the village below the castle held by William Fitz-Ansculf, but the smith would have been kept busy shoeing horses, making plough-shares and sharpening weapons. Although unrecorded, it may be assumed that iron-ore was extracted from the Dudley area and smelted with local charcoal.

2
The Middle Ages

The baronial system of provincial government established by William the Conqueror served that monarch well but plagued his successors. During the early Middle Ages the English nobility increased their political power through the acquisition of land, the basis of their wealth. A series of bloody but essentially local feuds and quarrels among a land-hungry aristocracy eventually resulted in a direct challenge to the greatest landowner of all – the Crown. Civil war (the so-called Wars of the Roses) erupted in the mid-fifteenth century and was largely played out across the Midland shires. It is doubtful whether such affairs of state infringed upon the lives of the mass of the common people – except, that is, when their menfolk were pressed into the local lord's service or their harvest was stolen to feed his mercenary gangs.

8 An attack upon a castle during the Wars of the Roses. Frontal assaults like this were rare. The usual practice was to beseige the fortress and starve the garrison into surrender.

The defeat of Richard III at Bosworth Field in Leicestershire in 1485 by the rebel army of Henry Tudor brought to a close a chapter of English history. Henceforth power would be centralized in the monarchy and warring barons would no longer send their private armies on murderous expeditions into their neighbours' territory. The Tudor and Elizabethan regimes brought stability and a certain degree of prosperity to a nation ravaged by decades of foreign wars, internal fighting and economic depression.

The Medieval period may be regarded as a transition between a pioneering people carving their livelihood from the wilderness and a mature nation embarking upon its great industrial adventure. During the two centuries following Bosworth the Midlands made slow but emphatic progress in terms of urban growth, agricultural reorganization and industrial development.

People

The population of England more than doubled between 1086 and the early fourteenth century, from some 1¾ million to approximately 4¼ million. There were, however, wide variations in growth rates between one area and another. The villages of South Warwickshire were roughly the same size in 1279 as in 1086. To the north of the River Avon, though, hamlets in the Forest of Arden were attracting people throughout the twelfth and thirteenth centuries, as more land became available through woodland clearance.

By 1330 growth everywhere had probably ceased. It appears that the total number of people exceeded the means of subsistence and that new lands could not be brought into cultivation quickly enough to prevent starvation on a local, and sometimes on a national (as in 1315-17), scale. The effects of famines were cumulative in that a bad harvest meant skimping on seed corn the following year. This would itself mean a poor output and a further low level of planting in the succeeding year. Only a bumper harvest could pull a community out of this vicious downward spiral. In addition, any shortage of food must have reduced the physical resistance of the working people, thus exposing them to a greater risk from disease.

The population, weakened by malnutrition and disease, could not cope with the outbreak of bubonic plague in 1348. By the end of 1350 between one-third and one-half of the population of England had fallen victim to the Black Death.

The plague originated in India and swept across North Africa, Europe and the North Atlantic islands. Its toll was heaviest in the crowded towns and the densely settled agricultural districts. Thus in the Midlands the death rate was highest in the fertile areas of south Warwickshire and central Worcestershire, in the Trent and Soar valleys and along the lower Severn. In such areas villages lost between 40 and 50 per cent of their inhabitants. Within the towns of Leicester, Nottingham, Coventry and Gloucester the plague may have struck down as many as 60 per cent of the townsfolk. In the west of the

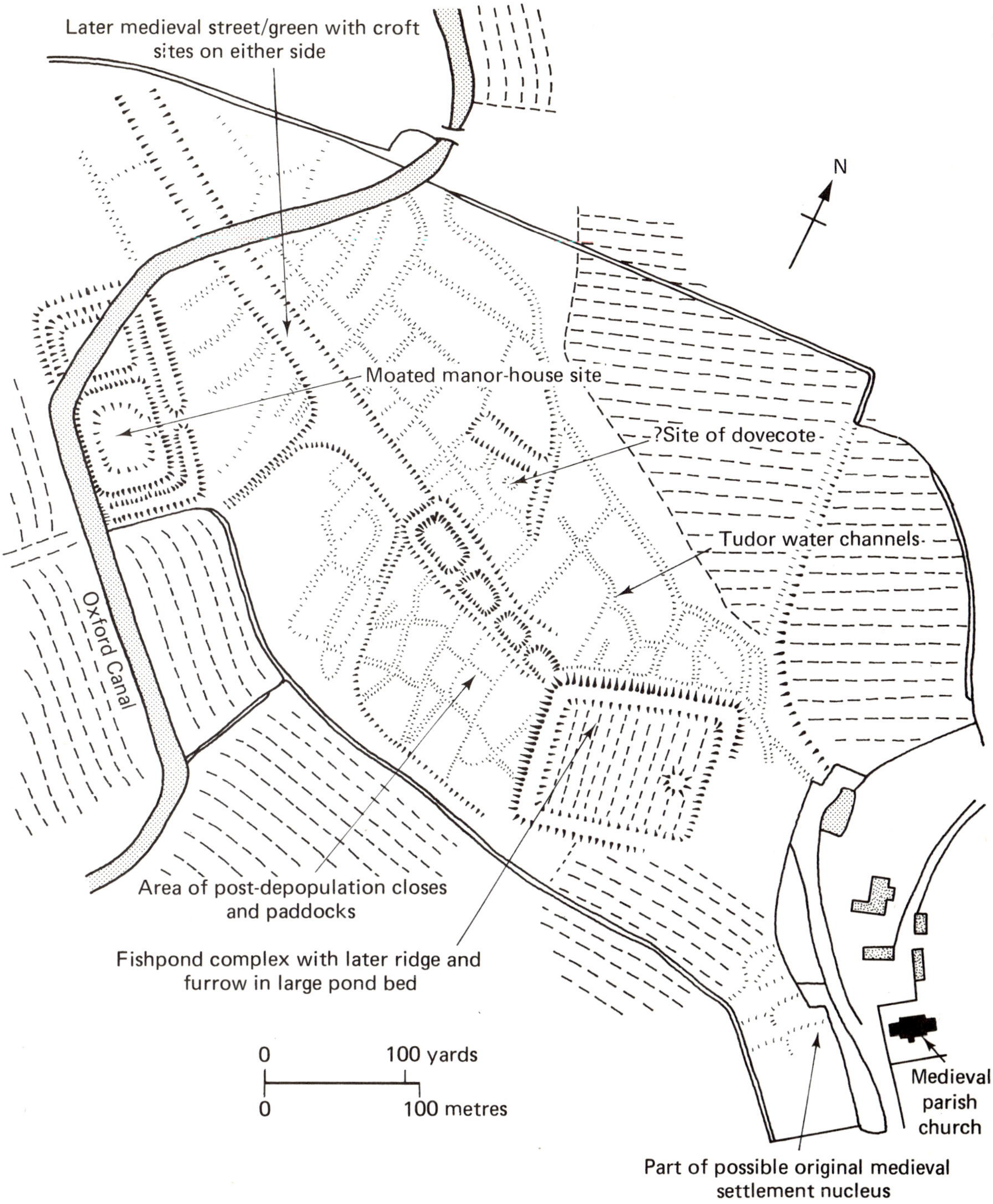

9 The deserted Medieval village of Wormleighton, Warwickshire.

region, however, the sparse population ensured that death rates were relatively low – perhaps only 15 per cent of the populations of Shropshire and Staffordshire.

The outbreak of the Black Death was so severe that it took many areas more than two centuries to recover from its awful visitation. The population of Leicestershire in 1563, for example, was still below its level in 1334. For the nation as a whole, the pre-plague figure of some 4¼ million was not reached again until 1600.

Children reciting a popular nursery rhyme unwittingly recall the calamity of the fourteenth century: 'Ring-a-ring of roses' (the tell-tale symptom of plague was a rose-shaped patch on the skin), 'a pocketful of posies' (the bag of herbs carried to ward off contagion), 'a-tishoo, a-tishoo' (the virulent pneumonic form of plague was characterized by sneezing fits), 'we all fall down' (death).

Certain effects of the Black Death are still noticeable today. Chief amongst these are the deserted villages, hundreds of which are scattered throughout the Midlands. It appears that few villages, apart from those on the frontiers of cultivation, were totally deserted as a result of the plague. The Black Death, however, did initiate a process of abandonment that gathered strength through the succeeding centuries.

Deserted village sites vary greatly in both size and state of preservation. Holyoak, in eastern Leicestershire, once boasted some 200 houses while Great Stretton, in the same county, numbered between 15 and 20. The site of the latter village is a tumbled piece of ground consisting of grass-covered platforms separated by narrow gullies. These platforms are the sites of peasant dwellings which, because they were constructed of mud and timber, have completely perished. Adjoining the village is the rectangular site of the local squire's moated manor house.

The locations of certain villages have been known for many years. John Rous noted 48 sites in Warwickshire alone in his history of England, written in 1486. Clues to the one-time existence of hamlets and villages are provided by manorial and ecclesiastical records, by lone churches standing amid open fields and by irregular dips and hummocks on the ground. Aerial photography in recent years has defined the extent of many villages, but their excavation and detailed mapping remains one of the greatest and most fascinating challenges to the Midland archaeologist.

The Medieval Countryside

The Black Death was not solely responsible for the abandonment of Midland villages during the fourteenth, fifteenth and early sixteenth centuries. Depopulation was largely a result of a massive change in land use, from arable to grass, stimulated by an increasing demand for wool.

Midland landlords, particularly the Cistercian monasteries, eager to cash-in on the sheep-rearing boom, enclosed the traditional open fields, evicted redundant villagers and either levelled villages themselves or let nature take its destructive course. Thus in 1498 William Cope, Treasurer of the Household to Henry VII, removed the occupiers of 12 farms and three cottages from his estate at Wormleighton in south Warwickshire. He enclosed 240 acres of arable with hedges and ditches and converted the new fields to sheep and cattle pastures. A total of 60 people were displaced, only a few of whom were required to tend the flocks. An indication of the profits to be made from specialized sheep-farming may be drawn from the sale of the estate of John Spencer in 1506 for £1,900 – a vast sum in the early Tudor period.

Such changes were enacted on a greater or lesser scale throughout the region until the late sixteenth century. By that time the disadvantages of extensive sheep-rearing (lack of winter shelter, the impossibility of achieving close grazing over such large areas, the difficulties of isolating diseased animals from the main flock, the lack of mature trees) prompted a reduction in field size by the planting of hundreds of kilometres of hedgerows. The planting and digging of hedges and ditches and their routine maintenance, in addition to other farmwork, required a considerable labour force. Hence many villages were able to retain their viability and even expand modestly.

The century before 1640 saw what the historian W.G. Hoskins has called 'the flowering of rural England'. The prosperity of Elizabethan England was reflected in the Midland countryside by a widespread programme of rebuilding. Independent yeoman farmers created the characteristic black-and-white houses of the West Midlands, while in the east whole villages (such as Colly Weston in Northamptonshire) were rebuilt of local stone. Large landowners built on a grander scale of course, befitting their position as favourites of either Henry VIII or Queen Elizabeth. Compton Wynates, lying below Edge Hill in Warwick-

10 Leys Farm, Herefordshire, an Elizabethan yeoman's house dated 1589. Richly-timbered buildings like this are characteristic of the Welsh border country and dominate villages such as Weobley, Pembridge and Eardisland.

shire, is recognized as one of the earliest and finest of Midland country houses. Finished in 1520 it was soon eclipsed by massive estates such as Burghley House (home of William Cecil, Lord High Treasurer to Elizabeth), which took some 30 years to complete.

The majority of Midlanders, the rural peasantry, continued to live in the dark, squalid and cramped dwellings of their ancestors. According to Hoskins 'these were generally two-roomed houses – a hall and a bower – built of a timber frame with walls of reinforced mud, the whole raised upon a rubble foundation. There were no glazed windows, and only one fireplace. The two rooms were not ceiled over, but were open to the rafters and the thatch of the roof.' Tied to the land and living just above starvation level, the lot of the Midland peasant had barely improved during the Medieval period.

11 The Green Velvet Bedroom at Hardwick Hall, Derbyshire: early seventeenth century. The tapestries on the walls were imported from Flanders and, like the bed curtains, served a practical purpose as draught excluders.

Markets and Merchants

The urban history of the Midlands dates from the Medieval era. Although certain towns, such as Ludlow, Shrewsbury, Dudley and Newcastle-under-Lyme, owe their origins to Anglo-Norman fortifications, most Medieval settlements began their expansion in the twelfth or thirteenth centuries with the granting of a market charter. Birmingham, for example, was granted, in 1166 the right to hold a weekly market every Thursday. The Lord of the manor, Peter de Bermingham, was also given permission to take a cut of the market's profits. Not surprisingly, his descendants clamoured for additional privileges for their village; these were forthcoming in 1251 with the right to hold an annual fair. Similarly, the urban development of Henley-in-Arden began with Peter de Montfort obtaining, in 1220, a charter for a weekly market on Mondays and the right to hold an annual fair on the feast-day of St Giles. (By 1296 the town contained 69 merchants who paid an annual rent of £7.93p to the de Montfort estate).

Once established, such markets grew rapidly. At first, they merely provided a place of exchange for the locality's surplus agricultural products and the town's simple manufactured goods. But as rural emigration swelled the urban population and the output from the town's workshops grew, the market expanded its sphere of influence and trading developed between nearby towns. A few of the larger settlements, such as Coventry, Leicester and Nottingham, had forged strong commercial links with Bristol and London by the close of the thirteenth century.

The granting of a market charter, however, was not a prescription for the instant success of all settlements. One of the most interesting features of the Medieval period is the number of villages which received charters, and seemed set for expansion, but could not maintain their growth in later years. In Shropshire, only 15 of the original 60 markets chartered before 1330 are still trading. As each landowner wanted to share in the growing prosperity of Medieval England, many markets were sited at unsuitable points and thus could not compete with towns which were located at the junction of important trading routes.

Markets not only promoted the growth of towns, they also gave rise to the merchant class. The rights extended to burgesses or merchants in the

12 The impressive Guildhall in the small Warwickshire market town of Alcester suggests the local importance of the merchant class.

Medieval Midlands varied from town to town. In those settlements dominated by a powerful baronial lord, like Dudley and Warwick, the merchants' privileges were relatively limited. But in towns such as Coventry, with an absentee landlord, the burgesses were granted significant freedoms in return for financial rewards. These liberties were extended through time until the merchant class was often powerful enough to regulate the production and distribution of a wide variety of commodities. In many towns, the guildhall (the seat of government of the merchants' associations) performed the combined functions of law court, taxation office, weights and measures department, bank, immigration office and building society.

Medieval Town Planning

In order to develop or strengthen trading privileges, and hence their income, landowners often rebuilt existing villages or planned additions. The Domesday village of Stratford was a minor bridging point over the Avon until it received its market charter from Richard I in 1196. Within 50 years the Bishops of Worcester (to whose diocese Stratford belonged) had laid out a new town, covering 44 hectares (109 acres), built to a gridiron plan with three streets running parallel to the river and three cutting through at right angles. A survey of the town made in 1252 records 'some 240 burgage tenements, besides about 50 plots of land, various shops, stalls and other holdings'. Similarly, the large rectangular market area and the adjoining streets of Newark were developed by the Bishops of Lincoln, eager for a share of the wealth that the charter of 1150 brought to the town.

Although the gridiron plan was utilized in Lichfield and Ludlow as well as in Stratford, the usual form of development was the single thoroughfare, broadened in its centre to cater for the market, with minor streets joining at right angles. Those towns located in sheep-rearing districts are characterized by an exceptionally wide central street into which flocks could be driven. Thus Cotswold settlements such as Moreton-in-the-Marsh retain market streets which appear too large relative to present town sizes. Similarly, the huge but magnificent market place in Banbury, now largely given over to car parking, betrays that town's continuing role as the premier cattle market of the Midlands.

With the onset of economic recession after 1300, the creation of new boroughs virtually ceased. Certain towns contracted in size (the partially infilled market places of Ludlow and Stamford indicate such decline) while others, having weathered the storms of the fourteenth century, proceeded

13 New Radnor, an Anglo-Norman planned town. The village, protected by its now-ruined castle (bottom left), was laid out in the twelfth century to a gridiron plan. New Radnor, however, was too distant from the Welsh border trading routes and it entered a period of decline which culminated in the nineteenth century with the removal of its market and law courts to Presteigne. The subsequent contraction of the village is clearly seen on the photograph.

to grow modestly through the remainder of the Medieval period according to the strength of local trade. Town planning, the deliberate building of new urban areas, did not reappear until the eighteenth century.

It is interesting to note that throughout the Middle Ages the larger and richer Midland towns remained roughly the same. The table below, however, does show that relative positions changed over four centuries; of particular significance were the inexorable rise of Coventry and the decline of Northampton.

Midland towns ranked in wealth order, 1154 – 1525		
1154-89	**1334**	**1525**
Northampton	Oxford	Coventry
Gloucester	Shrewsbury	Worcester
Oxford	Coventry	Gloucester
Nottingham	Hereford	Hereford
Worcester	Gloucester	Leicester
Shrewsbury	Newark	Shrewsbury
Hereford	Peterborough	Oxford
Coventry	Nottingham	Stamford

Medieval towns were small in both area and population. Only the larger settlements listed in the above table fully deserve the title 'urban'. The vast number of minor centres, with populations of less than 2,000, must have been very sleepy, coming to life only on the weekly market day or during the annual fair. As John Patten, a geographer, noted:

> The bustle of shire towns like Worcester was absent in these little unwalled market towns. Their short streets ran out into the surrounding countryside and their inhabitants were often as much concerned with the prices of sheep and corn as with the simple craft and service occupations which supplied the immediate needs of other townsfolk and surrounding country areas.

Within the larger settlements the merchant group had generally established its authority by the mid-sixteenth century. The burgesses' homes, located at the centre of the town adjacent to the guildhall and the market place, were usually built of stone and often had a piped water-supply. Although the narrow streets, alleyways and tall buildings suggest that the Medieval town was overcrowded and lacking in open space, this was not so – at least not in the wealthier districts. Behind the houses of the rich were long, narrow gardens and orchards. The map of early eighteenth-century Leicester shows that these open spaces remained for several centuries. Yet today, only fragments of evidence give clues to the existence of these central gardens. In the heart of Birmingham, for instance, the name Cherry Street is all that remains of the old cherry orchards.

For most people living in Medieval towns, however, life was short, hard and unrewarding. Houses were generally built of wood and mud (the last mud block houses in the Black Country were torn down at Lye in the 1950s), with thatched roofs, and were often destroyed by fire. Streets and footpaths were seldom paved and became a river of mud and slime in winter. Water had to be fetched from wells or streams. Pigs, chickens and rats shared the family home and, not surprisingly, terrible epidemics swept through the squalid quarters inhabited by the poor.

Certain of the larger settlements were enclosed by a wall. In some cases (Nottingham and Stafford, for example) earlier ramparts were strengthened and extended. Usually however, as with Coventry, construction began without previous foundations. Walls were not built simply for defensive purposes; rather they defined the extent of the town, as do boundaries drawn on a modern map. At no other time in Midland history were town and country farther apart. The wall not only physically surrounded the urban community, but also enclosed the outlook of the inhabitants. This produced in the inward-

14 Leicester in 1741 – the town had barely outgrown its Medieval form.

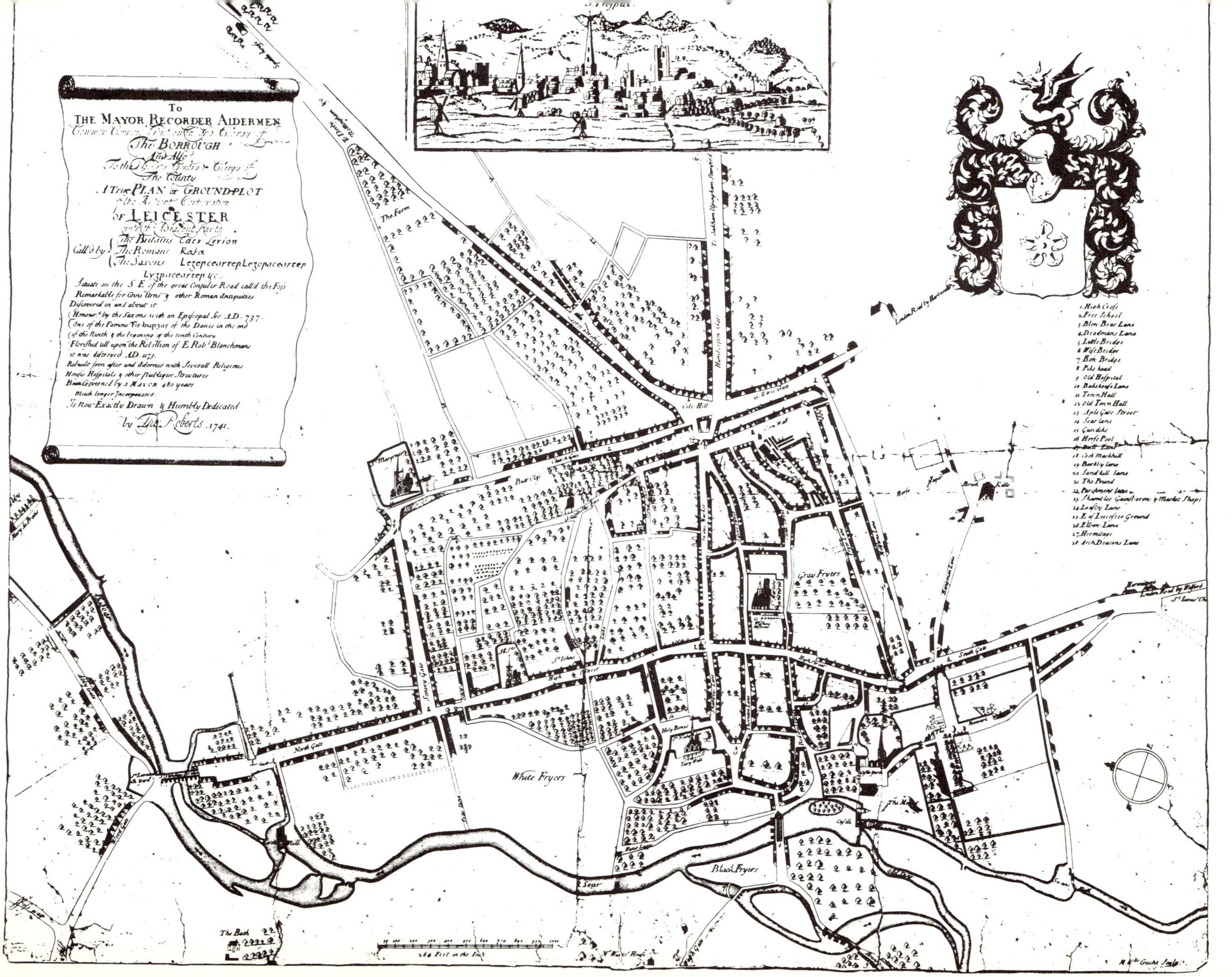
To
THE MAYOR RECORDER ALDERMEN
The BORROUGH
And Also
The County
A True PLAN or GROUND-PLOT
of LEICESTER
Call'd by The Britains Caer Lerion
The Romans Ratæ
Situate on the S E of the great Consuler Road call'd the Foss
Remarkable for Coins Urns & other Roman Antiquities
Discovered in and about it
Honour.d by the Saxons with an Episcopal See A.D. 737
One of the Famous Fir-burgar of the Danes in the end
of the Ninth & the begining of the tenth Century
Florished till upon the Rebellion of E. Rob.t Blanchmans
it was destroyed A.D. 1173.
Rebuilt soon after and adorned with Severall Religious
Houses Hospitals & other publique Structures
Been Governed by a MAYOR 480 years
Much longer Incorporated.
Is Now Exactly Drawn & Humbly Dedicated
by Tho. Roberts. 1741.
1 High Cross
2 Free School
3 Blew Boar Lane
4 Deadmans Lane
5 Little Bridge
6 West Bridge
7 Bow Bridge
8 Pike head
9 Old Hospital
10 Bakehouse Lane
11 Town Hall
12 Old Town Hall
13 Aple Gate Street
14 Soar lane
15 Gun dike
16 Horse Pool
18 Cock Muckhill
19 Berkley lane
20 Sand-hill lane
21 The Pound
22 Parchment lane
23 Shambles Gainsborow & Market Shops
24 Leasby Lane
25 E. of Leicester Ground
26 Elbow Lane
27 Hermitage
28 Arch Deacons Lane
The Farm
Cole Hill
Humberston Gate
Gray Fryers
White Fryers
Black Fryers
North Gate
South Gate
High Street
St Johns
Holy Bones
Castle
Soar
Margarets
The Bath
London Road by Harborough
London Road by Welford
Hermitage
264 Feet in the Inch

looking town dweller a sense of citizenship and belonging to a community that was perhaps the most characteristic feature of urban life in the Middle Ages.

The Origins of Midland Industry

During the Middle Ages the Midlands experienced a series of far-reaching developments in industrial activity. Initially, manufacturing was confined to urban settlements and controlled by craft guilds. The latter, through organizing craftsmen, supervising standards of workmanship and maintaining high prices for finished products, undoubtedly benefited infant industries. But, with an increasing demand for workshop commodities and the growth of national marketing, the guilds' restrictions impeded both increases in production and the introduction of new techniques. In particular, the 'closed shop' was a major source of annoyance to progressive merchants. This practice (of forcing craftsmen in certain occupations to work only in guild towns) prompted traders to seek cheap labour in the countryside. Thus, between the fifteenth and eighteenth centuries, a remarkable expansion of rural industry took place.

Within the Midland shires the major industry was the manufacture of woollen garments. At first, each district made roughly similar articles, but with a rising population (and hence an escalation of demand) through the Tudor period, competition between areas led to specialization. By 1600 fine woollens were produced in fulling mills located alongside fast-flowing Cotswold streams, while coarser stuffs, shalloons and serges were concentrated in Kidderminster, Coventry and Kettering. Witney in Oxfordshire was renowned for its blankets and the East Midlands for knitted stockings.

Hosiery knitting in the sixteenth century was largely centred in the stock-keeping communities of Sherwood Forest. Merchants supplied raw materials to the villagers who patiently knitted while tending their animals. The finished garments were collected by the merchant (or factor) on his next visit and sold in the markets of Nottingham, Leicester or Mansfield. Confirmation of the industry's standing in the East Midlands owes much to William Lee of Calverton who, in 1589, invented a knitting frame. Discouraged by Queen Elizabeth I because, it is suggested, she feared unemployment amongst the hand-knitters, Lee left in disgust for France. In the 1640s, after Lee's death, his brother returned to England with the patent and the framework knitting industry rapidly spread throughout the East Midland region.

Although woollen goods dominated the Medieval industrial economy, other commodities had achieved regional significance by 1600. The tanning of leather was an important process in Northamptonshire and south Staffordshire, lace-making had begun its long history in Nottingham, while pottery was produced around Burslem at least as early as 1348. The period after 1400 also saw the growth of the hardware trades of the West Midlands.

Settlement had previously shunned the heavily wooded Birmingham Plateau, but with the local working of coal and iron-ore in the late fourteenth century, merchants and craftsmen were encouraged into the small market centres of Birmingham, Dudley and Wolverhampton. Although the gap in size between Birmingham and Coventry was great (in 1397 the latter town's market handled over 3,000 woollen broadcloths, while Birmingham's totalled only 44), the Plateau towns were laying the foundations for future growth by specializing in various forms of hardware production. Soon after 1500, Wolverhampton and Willenhall were recognized lock-making centres and Wednesbury's nails were sent throughout the country. Scythe production commenced (and continues today) at Belbroughton in Worcestershire around 1560 and the needle trade of Redditch grew under the patronage of the monks of Bordesley Abbey.

By 1546 Birmingham's population numbered only 1,500 but John Leland, who visited the town at that time, found a flourishing community:

> There be many smithes in the towne, that use to make knives and all maner of cuttynge tooles, and many lorimers that make bittes, and a great many naylors. So that a great parte of the towne is mayntayned by smithes who have their yren and sea-cole out of Staffordshire.

Without any petty restrictions on production and trade such as were found in Coventry, Birmingham and the Black Country towns were magnets for families eager to win their living from the ground or practise their crafts in small workshops.

15 Early manufacturing: a tanner at work.

3
A Century of Revolutions

The period between 1640 and 1760 was an era of both experimentation and achievement in the Midland counties. In little over a century the region experienced dramatic and far-reaching changes in its political, agricultural, industrial, commercial and urban structure.

The Civil War and its aftermath brought to power a land-owning aristocracy who held sway over the region until the early nineteenth century. Farming

16 The newly rich: Josiah Wedgwood, the Staffordshire potter, with his family. A painting by George Stubbs dated 1780. Note the early push-chair.

became a respectable (and profitable) occupation for gentlemen, family fortunes being extended by forays into the commerical world. Men of humble background but of great ingenuity rose to positions of immense power and wealth through initiative in industrial development. And towns blossomed with their new-found importance as centres of economic and social life. The monuments to this period in Midland history are not only to be found in the great stately homes such as Blenheim or Chatsworth, in the delightful Georgian houses of Angel Row and Low Pavement in Nottingham or at the site of Abraham Darby's furnace at Coalbrookdale. They are also to be found at Bunny in Nottinghamshire, where Sir Thomas Parkyns, a typically self-sufficient (if somewhat eccentric) local squire, built a tiny school and decent houses for his tenants, designed his own home, dabbled in medicine and law, wrote a Latin grammar, but excelled only at wrestling; or beside the Dick Brook in Worcestershire, where a short walk reveals the industrial exploits of Andrew Yarranton, whose iron furnace, pack-horse bridge and flash locks lie almost hidden amid the pines and wild garlic.

Civil War and Restoration

On 22 August 1642, King Charles I raised his standard in a field behind Nottingham Castle and called upon his loyal subjects to rally to his side. It was not the most auspicious of occasions – the flag blew down and was trampled in the mud! Three weeks later Charles left in disgust, his army strengthened by fewer than 300 recruits. He fared better in Shrewsbury where, according to the author Daniel Defoe, 'he was received with such a general affection, and hearty zeal by all the people, that his majesty . . . raised and completed a strong army in less time than could be imagined . . .'.

The English Civil War, which raged intermittently between 1642 and 1649, was essentially a struggle for power between a proud and stubborn king (who could not accept that the monarchy no longer could rule absolutely) and an obstinate Parliament (who would not accept that an elite band of merchants could not attempt to rule absolutely).

Military action during the war was confined to a few set-piece battles (culminating in the decisive Parliamentary victory at Naseby in 1645), punctuated by a series of local but bloody skirmishes. Nottingham Castle, for example, was twice besieged by royalist forces from Newark. During the initial sortie royalist snipers climbed the steeple of the original St Nicholas Church to fire into the castle courtyard, before being driven off by rebel reinforcements from Derby and Leicester. On the second occasion, in January 1644, the castle garrison forced a determined royalist band to retreat, and 'for two miles they left a great track of blood, which froze as it fell upon the snow'. (Nottingham Castle was pulled down in 1651 not by the victorious Parliamentary forces but by the old garrison commander, Colonel John Hutchinson, for fear of 'Cromwell's poisonous ambition'.)

The 'battle of Birmingham' in 1643 graphically illustrates the growing importance of propaganda. A letter written by a royalist sympathiser from Walsall reports that when Prince Rupert's forces drew near to Birmingham, the townsfolk 'sallyed out of their workes', fired upon the advancing troops and called them names ('Cursed doggs, develish Cavaliers, Popish Traytors, etc!'). To gain an entrance through the barricaded streets, Rupert was forced 'to give orders for firing [burning] a house or two; but . . . he immediately gave order for quenching of the fire which was done accordingly'. A day or so later the Prince marched off to relieve the siege of Lichfield having given

17 A print depicting the decisive Battle of Naseby, in which Cromwell's New Model Army routed the Royalist forces.

'expresse command that no souldier should attempt to fire the Towne'. His orders, however, were not obeyed by 'some souldiers, as yet unknown, [who] fired the Towne in diverse places'. The letter states that Rupert sent word to Birmingham disclaiming responsibility, but 'the wind being high and the fire encreased, it could not be so soone extinguished as was to be desired'. How different is the account of the battle written by a supporter of the Parliamentary cause: 'The Cavaliers', he wrote, 'rode up into the Towne like so many Furyes or Bedlams . . . they shot at every door or window where they could espy any looking out, they hacked, hewed or pistolled all they met with, without distinction, blaspheming . . . [and] cursing most hideously.' As for the burning of the town, this tract places the blame upon Prince Rupert who, incensed at the resistance of the townsfolk, ordered the destruction of their property . . . 'and lest any should save any of their goods they had left, or quench their flames [the Cavaliers] stood with their drawne swords and pistols, about the burning Houses, shooting and indeavouring to kill every one that appeared to preserve goods or quench the fire . . .' Whichever account is true, some 87 houses were reported burned, 14 inhabitants and 16 royalists (including the Earl of Denbigh) killed and about 350 persons left homeless.

The legacy of the Civil War was neither the Interregnum under Oliver Cromwell (with its Puritanical fervour, its destruction of Anglican churches and its social experiments such as communal living) nor the Restoration of Charles II in 1660. Rather it was the 'Glorious Revolution' of 1688 in which Duke William of Orange was installed as king by a Protestant Parliament prepared to accept a monarchy which did not interfere with their commercial interests. Apart from the brief insurrection of 1745 in which Charles Edward Stuart (the 'bonnie prince' of Highland legends), as much as anybody the rightful heir to the English throne, led his army of Scots in triumph to Derby but eventually to bloody defeat at Culloden Moor, the political power of the ruling class of wealthy landowners and prosperous merchants remained unchallenged until the upheavals of the early nineteenth century.

The New Husbandry

In appearance, the Midland countryside did not undergo a revolutionary change between 1640 and 1760. It did, however, experience a remarkable series of developments made imperative by the food needs of an expanding population. Through the reorganization of farm holdings and the application of new agricultural practices, production of food was increased and loss of labour to the towns was largely overcome.

Enclosure of common land had proceeded for many centuries before the parliamentary enclosures which occurred mainly after 1750. In Leicestershire entire parishes were enclosed by agreement, but, as Hoskins wrote, 'the characteristic form of enclosure was piecemeal, a gradual process of nibbling bit by bit at the common fields, and most virulent around the fringes of the Midlands'.

18 This aerial photograph of the Wye Valley south of Ross-on-Wye shows clearly the regular, ordered agricultural landscape created by Parliamentary enclosure orders.

The Crown had resisted such changes prior to the Civil War, but the new government of landlords at the Restoration actively supported enclosure through co-operation amongst freeholders. By 1740, half of the county of Northamptonshire had been enclosed; in Leicestershire, at the same time, three in every five fields were bordered by recently planted hedgerows.

The early destruction of the Medieval open-field system was an inevitable by-product of the soaring demand for food in the century following the Restoration. Enclosure permitted the introduction of new crops and rotation patterns, the isolation of groups of animals for breeding purposes and a reorganization of farm holdings which enabled landowners to direct their labour force more effectively. After 1750, though, numerous Acts of Enclosure were passed by successive parliaments packed with land-owning members who

19 A map of part of Clayworth Parish, Nottinghamshire, drawn in 1749. The ancient system of common or open fields, divided into hundreds of narrow strips, still predominates although the process of enclosure has begun in the bottom right-hand part of the map.

PART OF WHEATLEY MA
CLAYWORTH COMMON
THE CASTLE FIELD
UPPER NORTH FIELD
LOWER NORTH FIELD
THE MIDDLE FIELD
THE UPPER HIGH FIELD
THE LOWER HIGH FIELD
THE CHURCH FIELD
Bull Dole Meadow
Long Starr Carr Meadow
Old Grange Meadow
Ley Field
Starings Meadow
PART OF GREALEY MANNOR
PART OF WYSTON MANNOR
THOMÆ DICKINSON
MDCCXLIX

were concerned not so much with agricultural improvements as with lining further their own pockets. The state's agents, the Enclosure Commissioners, by marking out the boundaries of new fields, determining the position of farm buildings and plotting the routes of new roads, transformed the ancient landscapes of whole parishes in a couple of years. The result was the characteristic Midland landscape of straight hawthorn hedges, regular field sizes and individual farms separated from the village centre, the monotony broken only by occasional stands of trees or the irregularities of earlier enclosure movements.

Of greater significance than the visual quality of enclosure was the loss of millions of acres of common land to a peasantry whose rights of usage stretched back before the Norman Conquest. Cheated out of his birthright, the landless agricultural labourer was condemned to a life of servitude; his village, stripped of its farm buildings and linked to a regional road network, ceased to be the focal point of parish life and became simply 'a place on the way to somewhere else'.

Agricultural improvements between 1640 and 1760 are normally associated with a few individuals who pioneered the use of new techniques. Andrew Yarranton of Ashley in Worcestershire (a remarkable man who directed his prodigious energy towards iron-smelting, tin-plating, canal construction and political economy in addition to agriculture) advocated the growth of clover

20 An engraving made in 1748 illustrating the various forms of plough available to the innovating farmer.

every third year to return nitrogen to the soil; Jethro Tull, who farmed near Crowmarsh in Oxfordshire, invented a drill to sow seeds in evenly spaced rows, while Robert Bakewell specialized in the breeding of animals. (At his Dishley Grange farm near Loughborough, Bakewell meticulously recorded the genealogy of his herds and carefully selected for breeding purposes those animals whose characteristics he wished to reproduce. Such methods produced the Leicester and New Leicester breeds of sheep noted for their high-grade quality wool, huge black carthorses and long-horned beef cattle.) The significance of these and similar improvements lies not only in what the individuals themselves accomplished, but also in their influence upon other farmers. Daniel Defoe, who journeyed through Leicestershire in 1725, described the commercialization of farming in that area:

> The whole county seems to be taken up in country business . . . particularly in breeding and feeding cattle; the largest sheep and horses in England are found here, and hence it comes to pass too, that they are in consequence a vast magazine of wool for the rest of the nation; even most of the gentlemen are graziers, and in some places the graziers are so rich, that they grow [into] gentlemen . . .

An Industrial Revolution

In 1709, Abraham Darby, working in the forested recesses of the Severn Gorge at Coalbrookdale, perfected the process of producing cast iron (a technique known in ancient times and partially rediscovered by Dud Dudley in the mid-seventeenth century). Consequently, Darby is often known as the father of the industrial revolution. But his innovation was only one of many industrial experiments which would eventually change the face of the Midlands.

Throughout the period between 1640 and 1760 a wide range of industrial products were manufactured in the Midlands. At first, many communities harboured a variety of craftsmen. Bewdley in Worcestershire recorded 56 non-agricultural workers in 1643, eight of whom were labourers and seven of whom worked on the river barges. The remaining 41 shared 21 different occupations, only one of which (the profession of 'gentleman') claimed as many as six members. In certain early industrial settlements, the inhabitants often retained other interests too. Thus John Waldron, a Belbroughton scythe-smith, kept a 'tippling house' and was 'a common tracer of hares in the snow'. Again, Humphrey Hill of Cradley was a nail merchant in the mid-sixteenth century who also sold ale through the Worcestershire countryside. Similarly, the connection with farming is shown in an advertisement of 1743 which offered, for a rent of £15 a year, a farm-house in Rowley Regis complete with barn, outbuildings and some 18 acres of land 'with a Nail Shop adjoining'. This co-existence of rural and industrial activities was common throughout the Midlands and nowhere was it seen better than in the Black Country nailing trades.

REFERENCES

By Figures, to the feveral Members.

1 The Fire Mouth under the Boyler with a Lid or Door.
2 The Boyler 5 Feet, 6 Inches Diameter, 6 Feet 1 Inch high, the Cylindrical part 4 Feet 4 Inches, Content near 13 Hogfheads.
3 The Neck or Throat betwixt the Boyler and the Great Cylinder.
4 A Brafs Cylinder 7 Feet 10 Inches high, 21 Inches Diameter, to Rarifie and Condenfe the Steam.
5 The Pipe which contains the Buoy, 4 Inches Diameter.
6 The Mafter Pipe that Supplies all the Offices, 4 Inches Diameter.
7 The Injecting Pipe fill'd by the Mafter Pipe 6, and ftopp'd by a Valve.
8 The Sinking Pipe, 4 Inches Diameter, that carries off the hot Water or Steam.
9 A Replenifhing Pipe to the Boyler as it waftes with a Cock.
10 A Large Pipe with a Valve to carry the Steam out of Door.
11 The Regulator moved by the 2 Y y and they by the Beam, 12.
12 The Sliding Beam mov'd by the little Arch of the great Beam.
13 Scoggen and his Mate who work Double to the Boy, 7 is the Axis of him.
14 The great Y that moves the little y and Regulator, 13 and 12 by the Beam 12.
15 The little y, guided by a Rod of Iron from the Regulator.
16 The Injecting Hammer or F that moves upon it's Axis in the Barge 17.
17 Which Barge has a leaking Pipe, befides the Valve nam'd in Nº 7.
18 The Leaking Pipe 1 Inch Diameter, the Water falls into the Well.
19 A Snifting Bafon with a Cock, to fill or cover the Air Valve with Water.
20 The Wafte Pipe that carries off the Water from the Pifton.
21 A Pipe which covers the Pifton with a Cock.
22 The Great Sommers that Support the Houfe and Engine.
23 A Lead Cyftern, 2 Feet fquare, fill'd by the Mafter Pipe 6.
24 The Wafte Pipe to that Cyftern.
25 The Great Ballanc'd Beam that Works the whole Engine.
26 The Two Arches of the Great Ballanced Beam.
27 Two Wooden Frames to ftop the Force of the Great Ballanced Beam.
28 The Little Arch of the Great Ballanc'd Beam that moves the Nº 12.
29 Two Chains fix'd to the Little Arch, one draws down, the other up.
30 Stays to the great Arches of the Ballanc'd Beam.
31 Strong Barrs of Iron which go through the Arches and fecure the Chains.
32 Large Pins of Iron going through the Arch to ftop the Force of the Beam.
33 Very ftrong Chains fixed to Pifton and the Plugg and both Arches.
34 Great Springs to ftop the Force of the Great Ballanc'd Beam.
35 The Stair Cafe from Bottom to the Top.
36 The Afh-hole under the Fire, even with the Surface of the Well.
37 The Door-Cafe to the Well that receives the Water from the Level.
38 A Stair-Cafe from the Fire to the Engine and to the Great Door-Cafe.
39 The Gable-End the Great Ballanc'd Beam goes through.
40 The Colepit mouth 12 Feet or more above the Level.
41 The dividing of the Pump work into halves in the Pit.
42 The Mouth of the Pumps to the Level of the Well.
43 The Pump-work within the Pit.
44 A Large Cyftern of Wood 25 Yards or half way down the Pit.
45 The Pump within the Houfe that Furnifhes all the Offices with Water.
46 The Floor over the Well.
47 The Great Door-Cafe 6 Feet fquare, to bring in the Boyler.
48 Stays to the Great Frame over the Pit.
49 The Wind to put them down gently or fafely.
50 A Turn-Barrel over the Pit, which the Line goes round, not to flip.
51 The Gage-Pipe to know the Depth of the Water within the Boyler.
52 Two Cocks within the Pit to keep the Pump work moift.
53 A little Bench with a Bafs to reft when they are weary.
54 A Man going to Replenifh the Fire.
55 The Peck-Ax and Proaker.
56 The Centre or Axis of the Great Ballanc'd Beam. *that Vibrates 12 times in a Minute & each stroke lifts 10 Gall of water 51 yards perpend.*

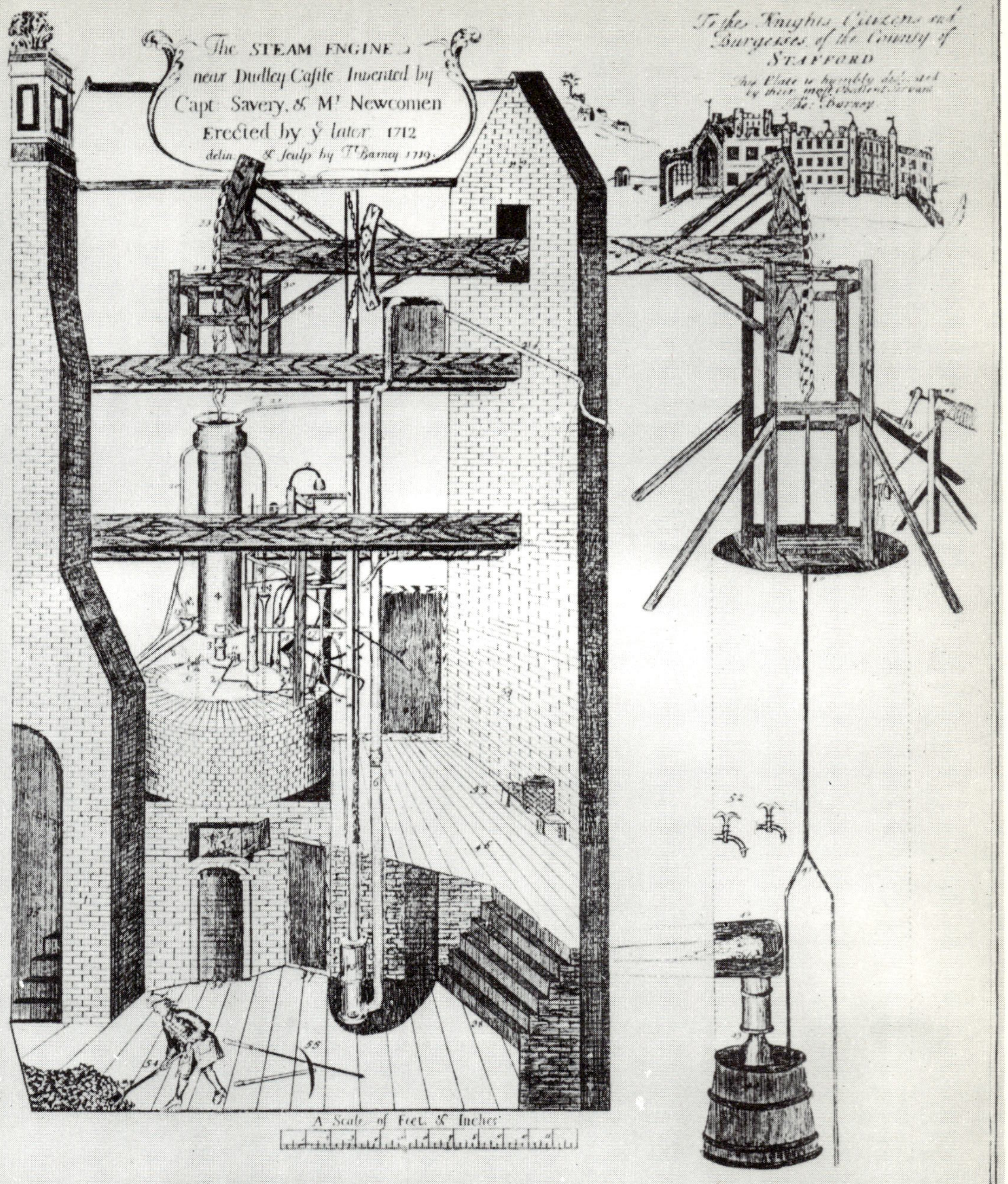

Nail-making probably originated in Elizabethan times amongst local farming communities, who turned to the trade both to satisfy their own needs and to supplement their income from agricultural pursuits. The industry spread rapidly through the small coalfield villages of south Staffordshire during the seventeenth century, as coal increasingly replaced charcoal in the forging of iron. Confirmation of the industry's location came with the introduction of the slitting mill, one of the most significant mechanical inventions in the history of industrial activity in the Midlands. The slitting process (by which rolled iron plates were sliced into long rods by means of a set of rollers) depended upon water-power; the many streams that flowed off the Birmingham Plateau were ideal for this purpose. (Old corn mills were often converted to iron-slitting, although Burstleholme Mill near Wednesbury, which was in the hands of John Simcox, an ironmonger, in 1663, produced both corn and iron rods when it was sold in 1709.) By the mid-eighteenth century nailing was concentrated in the Stour valley, iron rod being supplied principally by the slitting mills of Stourton, Kinver, Whittington and Wolverley. By 1760 these mills probably supported upwards of 5,000 men, women and children scattered in small villages and isolated smallholdings throughout south Staffordshire and north-east Worcestershire. A similar number of nailers operated with rod supplied by the Tame mills. Arthur Young, passing along the main road from West Bromwich to Birmingham in 1776, found it 'for five or six miles . . . one continued village of nailers'.

Nailing also illustrates another common theme in early eighteenth century industrial history, that is, the rise of both the factor and the industrial capitalist. The factor prospered in those trades which were essentially small-scale and widely scattered. With the growth of both domestic and international markets after 1700 it became necessary to obtain some degree of co-ordination within particular industries. Increased specialization meant that different processes were conducted at separate locations. It was the factor's job, for example, to ensure that iron rod reached a nailer at the required time, that ample forge coke was delivered to his 'shop', that collection of the finished product was made in time to reach the distributor as promised, and so on. In short, the factor performed the function of a conveyor belt in a modern factory. Factoring was both a blessing and a curse upon the trades with which it was involved. It ensured the smooth running of an industry and gave employment to hundreds of labourers who could not afford to purchase their own raw materials or market their goods. But, by separating groups of workers, it prevented their coming together to agitate for better pay and conditions.

The industrial capitalist differed from the factor in two ways. First, he owned the total productive capacity of his business and, second, he usually employed labour directly. His power was greatest in those industries which

21 Diagram of an early steam engine used for pumping water from deep coal workings.

required considerable capital expenditure. Coal-mining, for example, was conducted on a small scale until the introduction of the Newcomen steam-engine in the first quarter of the eighteenth century. Such equipment demanded heavy capital investment and the fortunes of the Griff colliery in Warwickshire indicate the difficulties involved with shifting from labour-intensive to capital-intensive modes of production. By 1725, Griff possessed two Newcomen engines for which a combined rent of £300 per year was paid. The strain of paying such a sum was too great; between July and September 1728, the business lost £290 and was forced to cease operations. The two engines were dismantled and sold. Such problems were experienced for many years: in 1800, Alexander Brodie, a Shropshire colliery owner, reported that an engine and other tackle for one of his mines had cost him at least £1,500.

22 The Iron Bridge (1779), cast by the Coalbrookdale Company to span the River Severn in Shropshire.

By that time, however, the demand for coal was great enough to cover such a large outlay of capital.

For those enterprises capable of withstanding the shock of successive injections of family money into their businesses, the early eighteenth century was a boom period. The Darbys of Coalbrookdale, for example, turned out 200 tons of iron in 1710. By 1760 production amounted to nearly 2,000 tons, some 1,000 workers were employed and the company had extended its interests to every part of the productive process, from the mining of coal and iron to the manufacture of pots and pans. Many family concerns grew from humble beginnings to positions of wealth and influence. Richard Foley, the son of a poor nailer, was born near Dudley around 1580 and appears to have practised his father's trade until the 1620s, when he leased Hyde House Mill at Kinver and introduced the slitting process into the Midland counties. After his death in 1657, his son, Thomas, greatly expanded the iron-making business. The Foley family thereafter prospered: it was raised to the peerage in 1712 and its status confirmed by the building of a country seat at Witley Court in Worcestershire, now an empty shell but justly famous for its incredible Baroque chapel.

'Paradise Restored'

In the early eighteenth century, Birmingham and towns which had progressed along similar lines, like Wolverhampton and Nottingham, were still far from being industrial communities. The 1731 map of Birmingham shows that it was still a country town. Many inhabitants worked smallholdings in the adjacent fields or grazed their animals on the surviving common land which surrounded the built-up area. In such towns, Medieval districts remained with their 'broad, badly-kept gutters . . . footpaths in bad repair . . . streets teeming with large round stones, laid in with gravel . . . constables few . . . heaps of rubbish plentiful . . .'. Yet by 1730 many Midland towns also had elegant Georgian squares that rang with the sound of carriages driven by uniformed retainers, and streets such as Temple Street, in Birmingham, in which a house was advertised in 1747 as having:

> . . . four Rooms on each floor . . . good cellaring and vaults, Brew-house and Stable with an entire Garden walled, and the walls covered with Fruit Trees . . . together with a pleasant Terrace Walk, and Summer-house with Sash'd Windows and Sash'd doors, adjoining to the open Fields . . . and all necessary conveniences.

Thus Nottingham to Thomas Baskerville, who visited in the 1680s, was . . . 'Paradise Restored, for here you find large streets, fair built houses, fine women, and many coaches rattling about, and their shops full of merchantable goods'. Derby, according to Daniel Defoe on his travels, was 'a fine and beautiful, and pleasant town; it has more families of gentlemen in it than is usual in towns so remote, and therefore there is a great deal of good and some gay company'. And Birmingham, in the eyes of William Hutton, who had deserted his apprenticeship in the Nottingham stocking trade:

> . . . rose in a style of elegance. Thatch, so plentiful in other towns, was not to be met with in this. I was much surprised at the place, but more at the people. They were a species I had never seen; I had been among dreamers, but now I saw men awake: their very step along the street showed alacrity . . . I had seen faces elsewhere tinctured with an idle gloom void of meaning, but here, with a pleasing alertness . . . I was treated with an easy freedom by all, and with marks of favour by some. Hospitality seemed to claim this happy people for her own.

Defoe's journal, packed with references to commercial activity, indicates that the marked increase in prosperity in Midland towns during the 1640-1760 period was caused not only by an expansion of industrial activity. Thus Northampton, 'the handsomest and best-built town in all this part . . . is counted the centre of all the horse-markets and horse-fairs in England, there being here no less than four fairs in a year'; Worcester 'is very full of people, and the people generally esteemed very rich, being full of business, occasioned chiefly by the clothing trade'; Shrewsbury 'is a great market for Welch flannel which the factors buy up of the poor Welch people . . . and thence it is sent to London'; and even little Atherstone was 'famous for a great cheese fair' held in September.

All of these commercial developments were reflected in an expansion of the market function within the major towns. As the population soared, new properties were added which specialized in a particular trade. These are shown in the 1731 plan of Birmingham by street names: Corn Cheaping, Cock Street, Mercer Street and Beast Market. Similarly, the early eighteenth century saw the growth of shopping streets leading off from the market area around the Bull Ring. Birmingham was already displaying, in a simple form, one of the major features of the modern city — the division of land into specialist zones.

23 Birmingham in 1731.

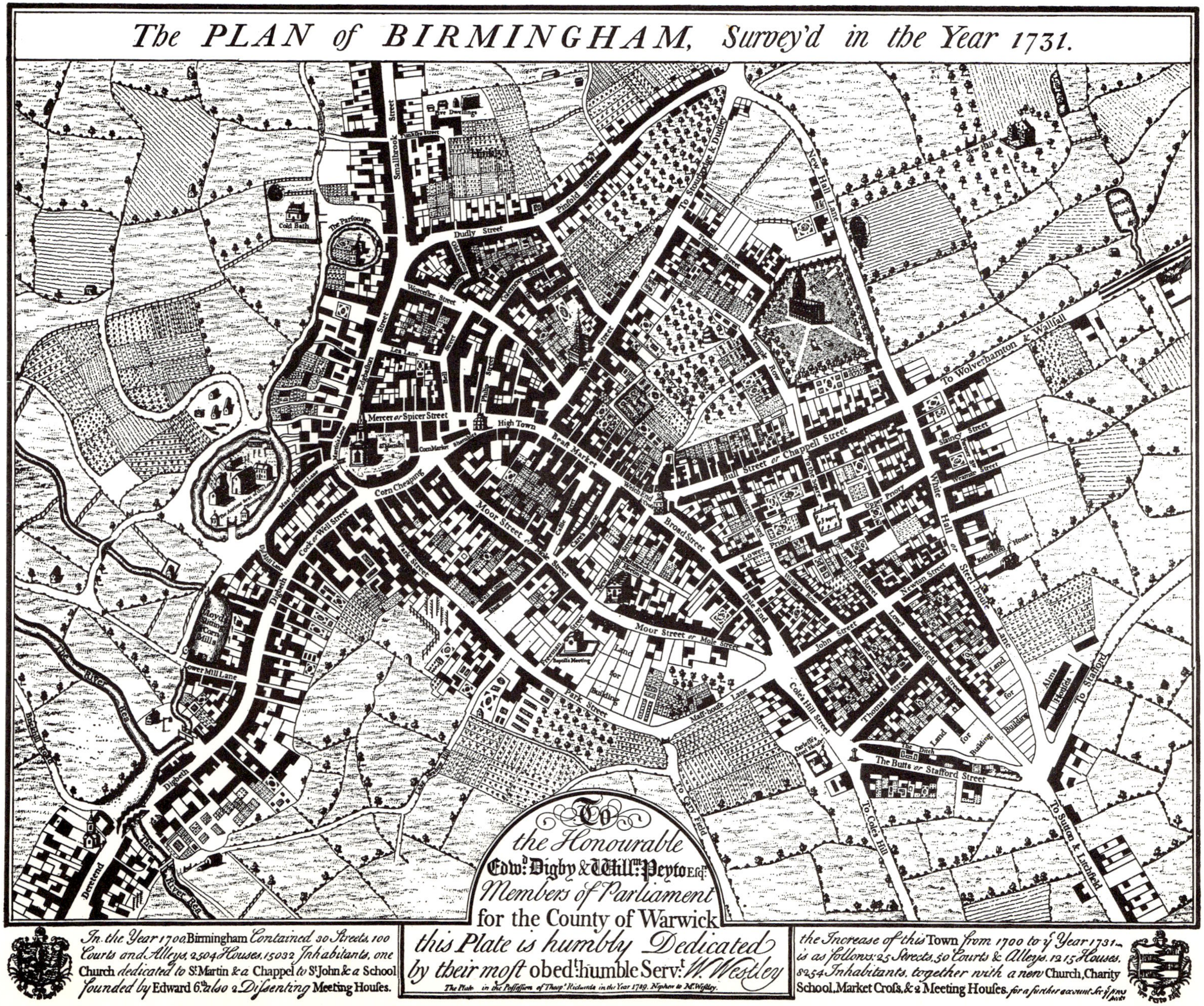
The PLAN of BIRMINGHAM, Survey'd in the Year 1731.
To the Honourable Edw.d Digby & Will.m Peyto Esq.rs Members of Parliament for the County of Warwick this Plate is humbly Dedicated by their most obed.t humble Serv.t W. Westley
The Plate in the Possession of Theop.s Richards in the Year 1789. Nephew to M.r Westley.
In the Year 1700 Birmingham Contained 30 Streets, 100 Courts and Alleys, 2504 Houses, 15032 Inhabitants, one Church dedicated to S.t Martin & a Chappel to S.t John & a School founded by Edward 6.th also 2 Dissenting Meeting Houses.
the Increase of this Town from 1700 to y.e Year 1731 is as follows: 25 Streets, 50 Courts & Alleys, 1215 Houses, 8254 Inhabitants, together with a new Church, Charity School, Market Cross, & 2 Meeting Houses.
Smallbrook Street
Dudly Street
Pinfold Street
To Stourbridge & Dudley
New Hall Lane
Temple Street
Temple Row
To Wolverhampton & Wallsall
The Parsonage
Cold Bath
Worcester Street
Edgbaston Street
Mercer or Spicer Street
High Town
Beast Market
Corn Market
Corn Cheaping
Cock or Well Street
Moor Street
Park Street
Bull Street or Chappell Street
Broad Street
Dale End
Moor Street or Mole Street
White Hall or Steel house Lane
John Street
Coles Hill Street
Thomas Street
Lichfield Street
Lower Lichfield Street
Land for Building
The Butts or Stafford Street
To Coles Hill
To Sutton & Litchfield
To Stafford
To Cary Field
Lower Mill Lane
Digbeth
Deretend
River Rea

4
A Beginning and an End

James Boswell, accompanying Dr Johnson on a tour of the Soho Manufactory in 1776, was rewarded with an epigram freshly coined by their host, Matthew Boulton: 'I sell here, Sir, what all the world desires to have – Power'! James Watt's steam-engine did not change the face of the Midlands, but it did hasten the shift from a society based on man-power to an economy driven by machinery. By 1832, the focus of social, economic and political activity had passed from the countryside to the towns, from agricultural pursuits to industrial enterprise.

The end of the old order was not achieved, as in France, by revolutionary activity, or by parliamentary legislation; rather, it was attained by a quickening of the pace of change apparent through the century preceding 1760. The control exercised by the land-owning aristocracy would eventually pass to the urban middle-class, the demands of industrialists would be quickly met by new forms of transport, a new system of industrial production and increased supplies of money, while the needs of the poor – for better housing, basic welfare facilities and secure employment – would go unheeded.

For some observers the emerging industrial society was to be welcomed and applauded. Thus:

> Soho! – where GENIUS and the ARTS preside,
> EUROPA's wonder and BRITTANIA's pride;
> Thy matchless works have raised Old England's fame;
> THINE! ever blended with a BOULTON's name.

Again, in the paintings of Joseph Wright of Derby, an artist fascinated by the strength of the new machinery, the interiors of workshops are depicted as intimate, domestic scenes, radiating warmth and prosperity. Other commentators, though, wrote of the destruction wrought by industrialization. Uvedale Price, for example, describing the cotton mills of the Derwent valley in Derbyshire, protested that 'nothing can equal them for the purpose of dis-beautifying an enchanting piece of scenery'. And the comment of an American, C. Edwards

24 Industry in the countryside: this smelting works in Middleton Dale, Derbyshire, seems to be in harmony with its surroundings.

Lester, who visited England in the 1830s, may serve as a comment on the age: 'I have seen more magnificence than I ever wish to see in my own country, and more wretchedness than I ever supposed could exist.'

'Not the Most Civilized of the Human Race'

Despite the far-reaching changes of the previous century, the majority of Midlanders in 1760 lived in a world restricted to their village and the nearest market town. Travel was slow, expensive and difficult over a road network that had changed little from Roman times. As the historian Harold Perkin remarked: 'Since the Romans left there had been little road building as distinct from repairing – which chiefly meant throwing gravel, broken stone, rubble or whatever materials came to hand into the worse ruts and potholes. They were, quite literally and legally, beaten tracks.'

The state of such roads was extremely bad. The writer Arthur Young reported in 1774 that 'the roads of Oxfordshire were in a condition formidable to the bones of all who travelled on wheels', while a traveller in Leicestershire wrote:

> In my journey to London, I passed from [Market] Harborough to Northampton, and well was it that I was in a light Berlin, and six good horses, or I might have been overlaid . . . But for fear of life and limb, I walked several miles on foot, met 20 waggons tearing their goods to pieces, and the drivers cursing and swearing . . .

Per Kalm, a Swedish minister who passed through the Midlands in the 1740s, noted: 'That the roads are so deep seems to come from this, that . . . very large waggons are used with many horses in front, on which waggons a very heavy load is laid. Through many years' driving, these waggons seem to have eaten down into the ground, and made the road so deep.' Street names like Drews Holloway in Halesowen and Holloway Head in Birmingham recall such eighteenth-century road conditions.

Most people who could afford it travelled on horseback. But the horse was an expensive animal, costing £20 to £50 (the equivalent of two to three years' wages for a labourer) in the 1770s. The stage coach had been introduced in the reign of Charles I (1625-49), but was not particularly common until after 1790. A journey from London to Birmingham took two days in summer (four in winter) and cost around £2.00 – about two months' wages for a labourer. Coach travel did not necessarily guarantee a smooth ride: James Boswell, the future biographer of Dr Johnson, shared a chaise with a Mr Stewart from Edinburgh to London in 1762. Between Stamford and Stilton a young, unruly horse ran away with the driver, the chaise overturned and 'Stewart's head and my arm were somewhat hurt'.

The heroes of road transport in the late eighteenth century were the waggoners – a tough, hard-drinking breed, 'not the most civilized of the human race'. They drove massive carts pulled by teams of eight horses, or led gangs of 30 or 40 packhorses, laden with coal from the Black Country collieries, clay destined for the Potteries, wool from the Derbyshire hills bound for Manchester or iron-ore from the Forest of Dean. A waggoner's life was hard and often dangerous. Besides the hazards of the weather, the deep mud-filled potholes, road surfaces liable to give way without warning and the threat from highwaymen and footpads, there was the constant danger of overturning. In January 1745, the local Birmingham paper, *Aris's Gazette,* recorded:

> On Wednesday last, a Man who was turning a loaded Waggon from the High Street . . . by the sudden Motion of the Waggon he was knock'ed down by the Shafts, and the Wheels going over him, he received so much Hurt that he died in an Hour afterwards.

This was a common occurrence.

25 An early coaching bill.

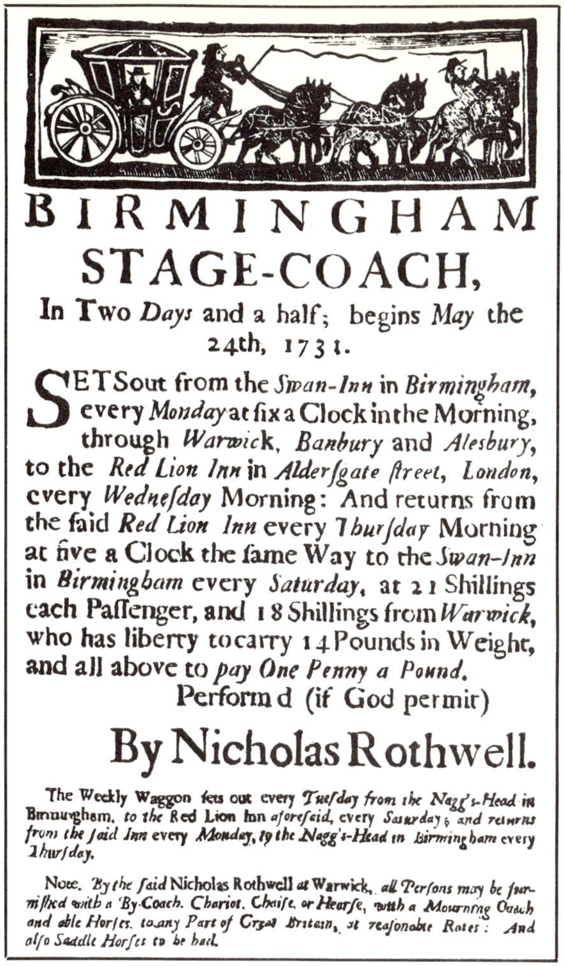

BIRMINGHAM STAGE-COACH,

In Two *Days* and a half; begins *May* the 24th, 1731.

SETS out from the *Swan-Inn* in *Birmingham*, every *Monday* at ſix a Clock in the Morning, through *Warwick*, *Banbury* and *Alesbury*, to the *Red Lion Inn* in *Alderſgate ſtreet*, *London*, every *Wedneſday* Morning: And returns from the ſaid *Red Lion Inn* every *Thurſday* Morning at five a Clock the ſame Way to the *Swan-Inn* in *Birmingham* every *Saturday*, at 21 Shillings each Paſſenger, and 18 Shillings from *Warwick*, who has liberty to carry 14 Pounds in Weight, and all above to *pay One Penny a Pound.*

Perform'd (if God permit)

By Nicholas Rothwell.

The Weekly Waggon ſets out every *Tueſday from the Nagg's-Head in* Birmingham, *to the* Red Lion Inn *aforeſaid, every Saturday; and returns from the ſaid Inn* every *Monday, to the Nagg's-Head in Birmingham* every *Thurſday.*

Note. *By the ſaid* Nicholas Rothwell at Warwick, *all Perſons may be furniſhed with a By-Coach, Chariot, Chaiſe, or Hearſe, with a Mourning Coach and able Horſes, to any Part of Great Britain, at reaſonable Rates: And alſo Saddle Horſes to be had.*

26 An eighteenth-century waggoner driving his massive load.

Canal Mania

In 1760, the average price of coal in West Bromwich was 35 pence per ton, but eight kilometres (five miles) away, in Birmingham, the cost varied between 55 and 60 pence per ton. The expense of moving heavy or bulky goods by road over more than a short distance was prohibitive. By 1769, Birmingham had been connected by canal to the South Staffordshire Coalfield. The first boat-load of coal was met by crowds of people. R.K. Dent, a Victorian historian, wrote that 'there was a sort of holiday kept on the occasion. Bonfires blazed on the wharfs, bands of music played, and there was general rejoicing.' No wonder people celebrated – overnight the price of coal in Birmingham halved!

Canal construction in the Midlands commenced in 1766 with the building of the celebrated Grand Trunk Canal which joined the Trent and Mersey rivers by way of the Potteries, thus cutting the cost of transporting china clay from Liverpool to the Etruria pottery works of Josiah Wedgwood. The success of this scheme prompted a spate of canal developments. During the great boom in industrial production in the 1790s, over 50 Canal Acts were passed and shares in construction companies changed hands at huge prices. By 1800, canals linked all of the larger manufacturing centres with the Midland coalfields and, via the river systems, with the major ports of London, Liverpool, Hull and Bristol. After that date, numerous spurs and branches joined individual factories and minor towns to the main canal network. Birmingham, in 1820, boasted more miles of canal than Venice!

The canal network was caused by the late eighteenth-century upsurge in industrial activity, yet it also caused this growth to continue. The importance of canals was due not only to their ability to transport cheaply raw materials, but also to their being able to distribute finished goods throughout a national market.

The introduction of man-made waterways added a new vista to certain Midland townscapes and stupendous engineering feats, like the canal which plunged into darkness under Dudley Castle hill to ship limestone from the caverns beneath the Wren's Nest or the bold flight of locks lifting the Stratford-upon-Avon canal on to the Birmingham Plateau, may still be marvelled at. Perhaps the most interesting feature of the canal age, however, was the creation of little ports. Few of these reached urban status. Their hectic moment of glory was soon over and Fazeley, Great Haywood, Autherly (all in Staffordshire), Braunston (Northamptonshire), Shardlow (Derbyshire) and West Stockwith (Nottinghamshire) slipped into obscurity in later years. Even those important centres which rivalled the old river ports could not maintain their individual progress once canal traffic declined. Elegant Stourport, for example, built between 1766 and 1772 at the junction of the Staffordshire and Worcestershire Canal with the River Severn, has only recently enjoyed a new lease of life with the growth of pleasure cruising.

27 Stourport in 1776. The town was built at the junction of the River Severn with the Staffordshire-Worcestershire canal and quickly grew into one of the most important inland ports in the region.

Money

Industrial and urban development in the late eighteenth century depended not only upon more efficient forms of transportation, but also upon the availability of capital. Just as the canals satisfied, in part, the first need, so did provincial banks satisfy the latter.

The origins of modern English banking lie in the seventeenth century money-lending activities of London goldsmiths. In the Midlands, banking originated a century later with the demands of local businessmen for both a stable currency with which to pay their workmen and a source of money for further expansion.

Certain industrialists who paid their workers in tokens (a form of coin which could be exchanged locally) eventually became bankers for a wider community. Thus the Finches of Dudley, a family of ironmasters and merchants who issued tokens as early as 1648, formally entered banking in 1791. Elsewhere, banks were established by successful businessmen who sought alternative outlets for their wealth. The Stevenson family, who made a small fortune in the woollen trade in London, returned to their home town of Stafford to open the Old Bank in 1777. Similarly, Joseph Berwick, a mercer, brought banking to Worcester in 1781, the Gibbons family of ironmasters set up a bank in Wolverhampton in 1783 and William Bentley, a draper, opened his bank in Leicester in 1781.

Many of these enterprises either failed during the Napoleonic Wars or were absorbed later into other companies. By contrast, the story of the first Birmingham bank is one of continuing success. In 1765, John Taylor (a wealthy manufacturer of small metal articles, buttons and trinkets) and Sampson Lloyd II (an ironmaster), together with their respective sons, formed a partnership with an operating capital of £8,000 and opened Taylor and Lloyd's Bank in Dale End, Birmingham. (The Bank shortly afterwards moved into prestigious new premises in High Street, a building not demolished until the 1930s). By 1780, the Bank, with a London branch in Lombard Street, was making an annual profit of around £7,000. (The early operation of the Bank, though, was not all plain sailing. During the economic difficulties of the 1770s, the partners filled bags with stones, topped them with gold coins, attached depositors' names to the bags and displayed them in the Bank's window, all to 'prove' to the public that the Bank was flush with money!) From such small beginnings grew Lloyd's Bank, one of the major British banks of the present day.

The 'Nursery of Ingenuity'

During the second half of the eighteenth century the primary processes, such as iron-smelting, were almost completely transformed into bulk-producing industries. This was very different from the development of the finished products industries (like nailing, the manufacture of tools or the production of leather articles) which simply multiplied manufacturing units as demand rose. Although technical innovations often accompanied increases in production, the transition from domestic to factory system depended not only upon further mechanization but also upon changes in business organization and management. Such changes are typified by the 'nursery of ingenuity', the Soho Manufactory built by Matthew Boulton at Handsworth (now a suburb of Birmingham) between 1761 and 1766.

28 Tokens issued by the Shropshire engineer John Wilkinson in the late eighteenth century.

29 Jedediah Strutt's cotton mill at Milford, in Derbyshire, built in the 1790s. One of the first iron-framed buildings, the mill utilised the water power of the River Derwent.

At its peak in the last quarter of the eighteenth century, some 700 workers were engaged at the Soho Manufactory in the production of buttons, coins, silverware, and medals plus an assortment of metal articles ranging from tooth-picks to ink-stands. Although each shop was eventually connected to a central power source 'which drove all the little lathes, drills and polishers within the works', and Boulton retained overall control of operations, the Soho enterprise was not a 'factory' in the modern sense of the word. Workshops were controlled by a department foreman who had a significant degree of independence, including the hiring of labour, the binding of apprentices and the distribution of the finished product. Some of these foremen retained outside interests. William Hancox appears in Birmingham directories in the late 1770s as a silver-plater; he also had an account with John Read, a Sheffield refiner of silver, yet during this period he was a foreman at Soho. In other words, Boulton operated rather like the traditional factor, the crucial difference being that he housed all of his workers under one roof instead of having them scattered in workshops throughout the district.

The reason for the development of the Soho Manufactory reveals a great deal about the evolution of the industrial economy of the late eighteenth century. Rather than stressing the value of Hockley Brook as a source of power, the relative cheapness of land in Handsworth or the possibility of undercutting his rivals through advances in mechanization, Boulton considered that the desirability of having his labour force 'under our eyes and immediate management . . . every day and almost every hour' was of prime importance.

A disciplined labour force was necessary if the benefits of a pronounced sub-division of work processes were to be attained. That such discipline could be achieved more easily at a single location was quickly recognized by Boulton, John Taylor (Soho's great rival in button production, who employed 500 workers in his Colmore Row Manufactory in Birmingham) and Josiah Wedgwood, the Etruria pottery manufacturer. Putting such a sytem into practice, however, was another matter. In their dealings with their labour force the businessmen of the late eighteenth century trod a wary path between the familiar traditions of the domestic system and the uncertain requirements

of industrial production. Under the former system both the craftsman and the unskilled labourer lived an irregular life. The historian David Eversley remarked that 'they worked no fixed hours. When trade was good they might labour seven days a week. When it was bad they were idle. When it was normal they worked a four or five day week, taking off Monday and sometimes Tuesday. Saint Monday was a local deity . . . ' A despairing Josiah Wedgwood wrote in 1776:

> Our men have been at play four days this week, it being Burslem Wakes. I have roughed and smoothed them over, and promised them a long Xmas, but I know it is all in vain, for Wakes must be observed though the world was to end with them.

The prevention of absenteeism, shoddy work and neglect of equipment took many forms. Boulton periodically feasted his workforce, most notably in 1791 on the occasion of his son's coming of age. This attempt to cement a personal relationship with his employees was characteristic of Boulton and stretched from a picnic he organized for some 200 workers in 1772 to the magnificent display celebrating the Peace of Amiens in 1802 when the Manufactory, bedecked with William Murdoch's new gas lights, saw firework demonstrations, copious drinking and the ascent of three Mongolfier balloons! A further feature of the operation of the Manufactory is important in this context. Boulton provided dwellings at Soho for certain of his employees. Undoubtedly such provision encouraged skilled artisans to work at Soho, but their immediate presence not only allowed their activities to be closely watched, it also developed a feeling of involvement in the continued prosperity of the enterprise.

Man and Machines

Chant no more your old rhymes about Robin Hood,
His feats I but little admire.
I will sing the Achievements of General Ludd,
Now the hero of Nottinghamshire.

Between March 1811 and February 1812, armed groups of Luddites destroyed over 1,000 knitting-frames in night raids upon East Midland villages. At the height of the disturbances no fewer than 12,000 troops were encamped in the affected counties, but such was the support for Luddism amongst the local population that few arrests were made.

Machine-breaking (whether the destruction of materials, looms, threshing machines, the flooding of pits or damage to pit-head gear or the burning of the property of unpopular employers) was an accepted form of direct action in the eighteenth century. Such methods were used to counteract wage reductions or to frighten strike-breaking labour and, particularly in those industries dominated by the small master whose investment was limited to a few machines, were often successful. Luddism may be regarded as a nineteenth-century extension of such practices, but on a far larger scale. This view, however, tends to ignore the more significant aspects of the movement.

Luddism has been traditionally presented as an outburst by unemployed hand-knitters who vented their anger upon the knitting-frame, the symbol of their distress. The Luddites who crept stealthily through the Nottinghamshire night, however, were artisans intent on protecting their interests. Only the frames belonging to manufacturers who had cut wages or were producing 'shoddy', that is, inferior articles were attacked. Knitters who had not served an apprenticeship, or women, were prevented from working. At Pentridge, 'after passing through the village, and examining the frames, and their holders, as to the work they made and the prices they received, [the Luddites] retired without any mischief'. In other words, the Luddites' target was not simply the machine, but the system in which customary rights and privileges were ignored. As the historian E.P. Thompson has remarked: 'What was at issue was the freedom of the capitalist to destroy the customs of the trade, whether by new machinery, by the factory-system, or by unrestricted competition, beating-down wages, undercutting his rivals, and undermining standards of craftsmanship.'

Just as Boulton was a bridge between the eighteenth-century master and the nineteenth-century capitalist, so too was Luddism a transitional conflict.

30 An engraving of 1811 depicting the Luddites as a wild band of cut-throats and arsonists.

On the one hand, it looked backward to old customs and practices, to the idea of the labourer being worthy of his hire, and to a belief in a government which would ultimately protect the working man from the unscrupulous manufacturer or the unjust employer should time-honoured methods fail. On the other hand, it reached forward towards a system of self-protection in which workers would unite to achieve those rights and conditions that employers and governments would refuse to grant them.

A Life Underground

Sir George Head, who journeyed through the Peak District of Derbyshire in 1835, noted that at Poole's Cavern, near Buxton:

> The limeburners and quarrymen have dotted the side of the hill with their extraordinary dwellings. These, from a distance, have a most unusual appearance, and resemble so many large ant-hills. They are literally burrows or holes, scooped out of the limestone rock, wherein the men live underground.

The occupation of caves was nothing new on the Midland scene. Hermits, monks and fugitives had occupied natural or man-made rock dwellings at Kinver, Dovedale and in Charnwood Forest, for example, from at least as early as Medieval times. During the late eighteenth century, miners for iron-ore, coal and limestone often lived either within or adjacent to their diggings.

The scale of mineral extraction grew dramatically during the late eighteenth century. In the earlier, shallow pits, coal was brought to the surface, by both men and women, up sloping planking or ladders. As the shaft depth increased, horse-power was used to wind up the coal. The horse walked round a circular track, pulling a rope to which was attached a wicker basket containing coal. The primitive construction of the winding gear made this an extremely dangerous operation (not until 1839 was wire rope introduced, thus cutting down the number of accidents caused by fibre ropes snapping).

The underground extent of these early mines does not appear to have been great. At Darlaston, around 1750, shafts were spaced no more than 46 metres (50 yards) apart; a plan of the area at that date shows 23 working pits in 4,047 square metres (one acre)! The reason for the small size of these collieries was partly due to the fear of fire and partly because minute pockets of land were owned by different people. In fact, this system increased the hazards of mining, because each owner attempted to extract as much coal as possible from his concession. This often meant (in the absence of efficient maps of the workings) tunnelling into a neighbour's pit, thus causing roofs to collapse.

At the coal face, the miner worked by candlelight, often on his knees in muddy water, sometimes following a seam no more than a few inches in width. Tubs of hewn coal were either pushed through narrow passages by women or drawn by blindfolded ponies. Children were used to 'pick over',

31 A view of the mouth of a coal pit near Broseley in Shropshire. This print, published in 1788, shows a two-horse power winding gin.

that is, separate the coal from the waste material. By contrast, the men who quarried limestone enlarged natural fissures into gigantic caverns illuminated by tar-covered brushwood torches. Typical of such an enterprise was the Lincoln Hill Mine in Shropshire. Worked from the early seventeenth century the mine, by 1801, boasted 'several prodigious caverns of limestone supported by stupendous pillars'. Such columns, often nine metres (30 feet) high and some six metres (20 feet) square, may be viewed (from behind the safety of iron railings) in the Wren's Nest Nature Reserve in Dudley.

The Fight for the Bill

A poem by Thomas Bancroft, written in the late eighteenth century, reveals the hostility between the aristocracy and the new class of manufacturers:

It is then, ye vain lordlings! ye treat us with scorn,
Because titles and birth your own futures adorn?
What worth to yourselves from high birth can accrue?
Are your ancestors' glories entailed upon you?
And is your lazy pomp of much use to a nation?
Are not parks and wide lawns a refined devastation?
But peace – 'tis presumption – too much would demean'em
To hold converse with upstarts, a vulgus profanem.
Their blood in pure currents thro' ages conveyed
It were impious to taint with the contact of trade.

In the same vein, James Watt wrote to a French friend in 1787 that 'our landed gentlemen reckon us poor mechanics no better than the slaves who cultivate their vineyards'. Again, Boulton and Watt, in their private correspondence, mockingly referred to John Taylor as 'the Squire', because of his purchase of the Manor of Yardley.

Although the more important manufacturers like Wedgwood and Boulton remained aloof from party politics, the above references suggest that the political power of the landed aristocracy would be challenged by the newly rich, but politically impoverished, urban middle classes. In fact, two movements swept through the Midlands in the late eighteenth and early nineteenth centuries.

The first of these was directed towards the reform of parliamentary representation. Before 1832, the rapidly expanding industrial centres were not recognized constituencies and could not, therefore, elect members to parliament. Rather, the House of Commons was packed with members who represented rural areas and who were often mere puppets of the country squires. Birmingham took a leading role in agitating for parliamentary reform in the early decades of the nineteenth century. Thomas Attwood's Birmingham Political Union, formed in 1830, was a predominantly middle-class organization, but it also enjoyed considerable working-class support. At the height of its campaign, in 1832, the BPU attracted 150,000 people to each of its meetings on Newhall Hill. A contemporary wrote that 'the voices of most of the speakers reached to the outskirts of the great assemblage, and to throngs on the roofs of surrounding houses'. With the passing of the Reform Bill in 1832, which gave Birmingham and other such centres a parliamentary representative as well as giving the right to vote to certain property-owning males, the impetus for further reform died down amongst the middle classes.

The second of the political movements of the period was far more radical in its nature. Heavily influenced by the French Revolution of 1789, the English 'Jacobins' variously sought a range of elementary freedoms (the universal right to vote in secret ballots, the right to join trade unions, to negotiate wages, to obtain cheap legal representation and to abolish primitive working conditions), although some groups undoubtedly also plotted to overthrow the monarchy and establish a republic. Every reverse in government fortunes was popularly acclaimed. Hence in 1812 when the Prime Minister, Spencer Perceval, was assassinated (by one John Bellingham, not for political motives but because of a personal grievance) the nation went wild. In Nottingham, for example, the crowd celebrated and 'paraded the town with drums beating and flags flying in triumph'. In general, though, there was little to cheer about. Successive governments responded to the threat to their position by repressive measures. Many simple but hungry workers were either executed or transported to penal colonies; revolutionary groups were wiped out or driven underground. Not until a century after the 'Fight for the Bill' were certain basic rights extended to the working classes of the Midland counties.

5
The Victorian Era

In 1837, at the beginning of Victoria's long reign, the mass of the population walked everywhere. By the time of the Queen's death in 1901, the working man often cycled or caught the tram to work while his employer might drive in a motor car (at a cost of about 1½ pence per mile compared to 2½ pence per mile for a pony trap). Victoria ascended the throne at a time when the Midland region was becoming an integral part of the national economy through the rapidly growing railway system. Her successor, Edward VII, was sovereign of a group of nations in which the products of Willenhall and West Bromwich, Kettering and Kidderminster were as familiar to the inhabitants of Calcutta and Cairo as they were to the people of London and Liverpool.

At the beginning of the twentieth century a range of new industries became firmly established within the region. Herbert Austin was producing motor cars at Longbridge near Birmingham, the General Electric Company had established a big plant at Witton in the same city, Dunlop tyres were made in Coventry, pedal cycles were manufactured at the Raleigh works in Nottingham and British Ericsson Telephones had been set up at Beeston. At the same time, the products of such as Jesse Boot (the Nottingham chemist), George Cadbury of Birmingham and John Player, the cigarette manufacturer (also of Nottingham) were household names. Yet other industries, including many upon which the region had based its prosperity, faced mounting difficulties. The cotton and silk mills of Derbyshire, Kidderminster's carpet factories, the brewing industry of Burton and the steel-making plants in the Black Country (as well as the traditional Birmingham workshop staples of brass, button, gun and jewellery production) all endowed the new century with an array of problems to which solutions are still being sought.

The later Victorians' capacity for failing to get to grips with fundamental social and economic problems was immense. Perhaps the fault was that their fathers appeared as giants whose works could neither be emulated nor criticized. The first generation of Victorians created the material framework of a whole new way of life, based upon town and industry rather than upon countryside and farming. Their lives were austere, their works monumental. The second generation built on their parents' work, but they lived in easier times. Perhaps it was symbolic that the first generation invented the locomotive while the second developed the bicycle.

The gentry owned the land, the farmers rented it, the labourers worked it. This was the normal pattern of agricultural organization in the Midlands during the Victorian era. The independent yeoman had virtually disappeared with the collapse of rural prosperity in the 1820s and the smallholder of the common fields had been enclosed out of existence by 1840. Certain farmers prospered as tenants of land their forefathers had owned, others quit the countryside and headed for the towns, most became labourers 'with no rights of cultivation beyond the garden hedge'.

Throughout the nineteenth century many thousands of country labourers left their homes and flocked to the industrial and mining centres. The life they embraced was harsh, but the world they renounced was often considerably worse. An agricultural labourer, even in years of relative plenty, was amongst the poorest of Victoria's subjects. Wages varied across the Midlands (being highest close to urban areas, where competition for labour forced rates up) but rarely exceeded 50 pence per week in the 1850s. Education, brief and interrupted during the summer months when children helped with harvesting, was sometimes available in tiny schools paid for by an enlightened squire and usually run by the local clergyman. Joseph Arch, the Warwickshire pioneer of trade unionism among farmworkers, went to the village school at Barford when he was six but left it after he had turned nine, to start work as a bird-scarer earning around two pence for a 12-hour day!

In addition to low wages, long hours and primitive working conditions, the farmworker's problems were compounded by his lack of security. Decent cottages were occasionally provided by the wealthier farmers, but in the main the labourer's home was a small, four-roomed hovel 'tied' to the farm —

32 The rural craftsman: Francis Payne, a Leicestershire cobbler, photographed in 1924 at the age of 98.

33 A factory with primitive hand-worked machinery — button making in Birmingham around 1860.

if a worker changed his job, he lost his cottage. Moreover, the labourer was usually employed only on a yearly basis. Many communities held fairs or 'mops' each autumn. The harvest completed, these gatherings offered a respite from the gruelling work, although their chief purpose was to provide a forum at which farmers would hire workers for the coming year. A song popular in the 1840s evokes an air of jollity in describing a mop:

So to the hirings we have come, all for to look for places,
If with the master we agree and he will give good wages.
There rolling Gin the hemp will spin and Sal will mind the dairy
And John will kiss his mistress when the master he is weary.
There's Tom and Joe will reap and mow; they'll thrash and ne'er be tired;
They'll load the cart and do their part, so they're the lads to hire!

But any labourer who remained unattached (either through advancing age, an injury or simply because of a fall in demand for hands) faced a long, bleak winter!

The Urban Magnet

James Dobbs, a singer and comedian, first performed his own song, 'I Can't Find Brummagem', at the Theatre Royal in Birmingham in 1828. One of the verses runs thus:

I remember one John Growse,
A buckle-maker in Brummagem,
He built himself a country house
To be out of the smoke of Brummagem.
But though John's country house stands still,
The town itself has walked up hill;
Now he lives beside a smoky mill
In the middle of the streets of Brummagem.

Dobb's theme was familiar to the audiences of all Midland towns during the nineteenth century. In 1801, Birmingham's population totalled 71,000; it had risen to 265,000 by 1851 and to 552,000 in 1901. Nottingham's population grew from 45,000 to 240,000 over the same period. Immigrants were attracted to urban areas like iron filings to a magnet; they usually walked, although some hitched rides with waggoners and a few, as the century wore on, used a portion of their meagre savings to take a train to their destination. By 1901 the Midland region was dominated by the Birmingham/Black Country conurbation, with other population concentrations in the Potteries and the towns of Nottingham, Leicester, Northampton and Derby. Who were they, these millions of immigrants who crowded into the Victorian cities?

Principally, of course, they came from the rural districts, perhaps expelled by enclosure or the advent of machinery, sometimes simply victims of the effects of a bumper harvest in Canada which sent wheat prices spiralling downwards. And thousands left because they could no longer endure the hardship and solitude of life on the farm. With their departure the rural community began to disintegrate. Local craftsmen, such as carpenters and blacksmiths, no longer had enough custom to remain in business, so they too headed for the towns. (The number of tailors in Rutland, for example, fell from 173 in 1851 to 63 in 1911, and that of shoemakers from 236 to 138.)

The new urbanites were not all from farming districts. Immigrants also came from those villages and small towns which had been the scenes of early industrialization but which, by the mid-nineteenth century, could no longer compete with mass production in city factories. Papplewick, Linby and Langwith, all East Midland villages with water-powered cotton mills, rapidly declined as Manchester's cotton industry expanded. Similar out-migration took place from those districts in which local coal and minerals had been worked out or were

34 Coal was the life-blood of the Victorian city. This photograph shows the precious fuel being collected from a railway siding in the Potteries. An army of boys with pots or buckets would always be ready to grab any fallen pieces.

considered uneconomic to extract. The lead-mining centres of Derbyshire (Wardlow, Rowland, Harlington and Priestcliffe) and the string of settlements across the Shropshire Coalfield (Oakengates, Wellington, Broseley, Coalbrookdale) were such examples.

The Age of Steam

As the nineteenth century progressed, steam-power promoted new and intense concentrations of large-scale industry which in turn demanded a large local labour force. Thus, as Hoskins noted, 'manufacturers threw up their mills, factories and works on the edge of existing towns, and their workers were housed in streets of terrace-houses built rapidly on the vacant ground all around the factory'. The end result was a formless and ever-changing jumble of wasteland, workshops, narrow streets and huddled houses. Midland towns were simply overwhelmed by the demand for space which could never be met within existing boundaries. Because the mass of townsfolk went about on foot, they had to live near to their work. The area of a settlement was therefore limited by the time an employee was able to spend each day in walking to work. It also depended on the distance that a loaded handcart could be pushed between different market stalls, warehouses, shops and separate workshops. Until a new form of transportation was developed, cities were forced to increase their central densities, which inevitably led to chronic overcrowding.

Steam-power sustained the industrial landscapes of the Black Country, the Potteries and the Erewash valley. And through the railway system it linked them together to form a regional economy.

35 By the late nineteenth century almost every small town in the Midlands had access to the major urban areas via the railway system. The railway network not only carried passengers to the cities but also brought urban-produced goods to compete with local products.

Railways, the dominant form of Midland transport for around 100 years, had a dramatic effect upon the appearance of Midland towns. Rugby, for example, remained an insignificant market town (noted only for its public school) until the arrival of the London and North Western Railway in 1838. The railway added a new quarter to the town – a 'rectangular gridiron pattern with monotonous terraced housing' – quite different to the old Medieval core area, centred on the market place and surrounded by haphazard, narrow, crooked streets.

The Midland station at Rugby was built more than 800 metres (half a mile) from the existing town centre. This was common practice. The railway companies not only needed many acres of cheap land on which to build but, in the early years, could not afford the massive costs of demolition and rebuilding. Many of these original stations, however, were too remote from town centres to service the growing passenger traffic. In 1846, the London and North Western Railway drove their track, via a series of tunnels, into New Street, the heart of Birmingham. Nottingham's central station – Victoria – was not built until 1898, when the last fling of the Victorian railway age, the Great Central Railway, was completed.

Midland traders, manufacturers and landowners welcomed the railway network. But, as the urban historian Gerald Burke pointed out, the railway boom did not only bring advantages to nineteenth-century cities:

> Vast areas of building were laid low to make way for swathes of permanent way, marshalling yards, goods yards, cuttings, embankments, viaducts and bridges and main-line stations . . . Dense smoke and fumes fouled the atmosphere, and the roar of engines and rolling stock at surface, below ground level, or, worse, overhead, grated ceaselessly upon the inhabitants.

Hard Times

A short walk from the centre of Birmingham in 1870 would have revealed the incredible gulf between rich and poor which characterized Victorian society. From the central commercial area with its stately Georgian buildings containing banks, insurance companies and other financial institutions, the traveller would pass through districts of mean housing, interspersed with workshops and factories, in which the urban poor eked out a living in overcrowded, insanitary conditions. A further few minutes would take the visitor into the leafy avenues of Edgbaston where the rich inhabited large, well-furnished homes attended by a platoon of servants. And between these two extremes existed a range of families striving to improve their situation. The skilled mechanic or watchmaker, the ironfounder or mason, by careful household management could attain a position of relative security; similarly, the clerk or railway official, the jeweller or master carpenter, through watching the pennies could achieve a degree of comfort that was out of his father's reach.

As the century wore on, such families could afford to rent or even buy a small terraced house. In drawing-rooms and dining-rooms gas lighting replaced candles and oil-lamps and, towards the turn of the century, many such homes boasted a Singer sewing-machine, a gas cooker and a maid-of-all-work. Eating habits were approaching the style of the twentieth century. Mrs Beeton's first cookery book, published in 1861, recommended a 'plain family dinner' of '1. Bubble-and-squeak, made with remains of cold beef. Roast shoulder of veal stuffed, spinach, potatoes. 2. Boiled batter pudding and sweet sauce.' An increasing number of convenience foods lightened the housewife's task. Bird's custard powder was made in Birmingham as early as 1840, Cadbury's cocoa was said to be a favourite of Queen Victoria and margarine became popular as a substitute for butter.

But there was no room for complacency. With no unemployment pay or social security, with no old-age pension and with high medical bills, a long family illness, the collapse of a business or the death of the breadwinner could hurtle a family into poverty. What had taken long years to accumulate could be wiped out overnight.

36 A poster of the 1830s indicating the hazards of life in the Black Country.

CHOLERA.

THE

DUDLEY BOARD OF HEALTH,

HEREBY GIVE NOTICE, THAT IN CONSEQUENCE OF THE

Church-yards at Dudley

Being so full, no one who has died of the CHOLERA will be permitted to be buried after *SUNDAY* next, (To-morrow) in either of the Burial Grounds of *St. Thomas's*, or *St. Edmund's*, in this Town.

All Persons who die from CHOLERA, must for the future be buried in the Church-yard at Netherton.

BOARD of HEALTH, DUDLEY.

37 A court in Stoke-on-Trent about 1900. The low building to the right contained lavatories and a communal wash-house.

38 Handbill advertising a Dudley sweep, about 1840.

J. HANSON,

(Late Kirkham)

CHIMNEY SWEEP,

TOWER-STREET, DUDLEY,

BEGS respectfully to inform the Gentry and Inhabitants of Dudley and its Vicinity, that he has commenced the above Profession, and hopes by his unremitting attention, to merit their liberal support.

⁂ *Small Boys, and clean Cloths, upon the most reasonable terms.*

☞ **BEWARE OF STROLLERS!**

The bottom of the Victorian barrel was particularly deep. Crowded together in small back-to-back houses, each only 3 metres (11 feet) square, with one lavatory shared between as many as 20 families and water available only from a pump in the street, the quarters of the poor were a haven for cholera, typhus and tuberculosis. Men worked long daytime hours, but it was not unusual for a husband to hold down an evening job as well. Most women worked (when work was available), which meant that infants would either be left alone or in the care of older brothers or sisters. Should the latter themselves be employed, the universal remedy was Godfrey's Cordial, a lethal concoction of opium and treacle which killed as many babies as it kept asleep. The prosperity of the Victorian Midlands rested upon such foundations.

Child's Play

Being a child in Victorian times was fraught with difficulties. Children born into working-class homes were often forced into employment at a tender age. After the 1870 Education Act, schooling was available for a number of such children in Board Schools. Instruction in reading, writing and arithmetic (with needlework for the girls and practical drawing for the boys) preceded the search for a job at the age of 13.

Child labour was a familiar feature of the Victorian Midlands. Although the shocking revelation of successive Children's Employment Commissions prompted the legal regulations of child employment in the mining and textile industries, plenty of trades remained unaffected. Thus in the 1860s an enquiry

39 Children at work: carrying clay in a brickyards, 1870.

reported that 11,000 children were employed in the Potteries 'under conditions which undermine their health and constitution'. Even trades which had been subjected to legal restrictions continued to defy the law. An Act of 1840, for example, prohibited the sending of climbing boys up long, twisting, soot-filled chimneys, yet, in the 1860s, this 'pernicious evil' was reported to be 'decidedly on the increase'. A Nottingham master sweep called Ruff explained that 'at first [the boys] will come back from their work with their arms and knees streaming with blood, and their knees looking as if the caps had been pulled off; then they must be rubbed with salt water to harden the flesh'!

Worst of all, perhaps, were the parents who employed their own children in their own homes. A lace-worker in Nottingham recalled that she stitched shawls from the age of three, often until midnight, her body pinned upright to prevent her falling asleep!

The employment of children was the lowest point of Victorian society. Parents were forced to send their children out to work in order to win a few more pennies to support the family; employers therefore benefited from an endless supply of cheap labour. And because of such competition for jobs, parental wages were kept to a minimum.

A middle-class childhood was an entirely different but nevertheless harsh affair. Children spent most of their early years in the seclusion of the nursery, from which they would be summoned at their cleanest and neatest to join their parents for a short period each day. Family prayers were often a daily occurrence and strict religious principles turned Sunday into a day which most Victorian children dreaded. A verse in the *Infants' Magazine* of 1868 tells of the sad locking away of toys on Saturday night:

Haste! put your playthings all away,
Tomorrow is the Sabbath day;
Come bring to me your Noah's Ark,
Your pretty, tinkling music cart;
Because, my love, you must not play,
But holy keep the Sabbath day.

Even very young children were forced to sit quietly and do nothing all day – except, perhaps, listen to improving reading and, of course, go to church.

School simply replaced the rigidity of family life. Boys were sent to boarding schools, the quality of their education being extremely variable. 'Improvement' was the order of the day – the headmaster of Rugby School wrote: 'What we must look for . . . is, 1st, religious and moral principles; 2ndly, gentlemanly conduct; 3rdly, intellectual ability.' Girls too suffered from a directed upbringing. The Taunton Report on Endowed Schools in 1867 stated the prevailing view: 'Girls are less capable of mental cultivation and less in need of it than boys . . . what is showy and superficially attractive are what is really essential for them!' For many middle-class girls, only marriage was an admissible goal.

Only 7.1 per cent of the British population aged 20 years and over was entitled to vote by the Reform Act of 1832. This proportion was increased to 16.4 per cent in 1867 (when urban working men were largely admitted to the franchise) and to 28.5 per cent in 1884 (with similar privileges being granted to rural males). Finally, in 1928, when women were given equal voting rights to men, the proportion rose to 96.9 per cent.

The struggle for power through the Victorian era, however, was not simply a question of gaining parliamentary representation. After all, Midland voters could only choose between Liberal or Conservative candidates, neither of whose parties championed the interests of the working man, despite their claims at election times! (In 1899, Richard Bell, Secretary of the Amalgamated Society of Railway Servants, standing for the Labour Representation Committee – the forerunner of the Labour Party – was elected MP for Derby. Although Bell could claim to be the Midlands' first Labour Member, he was virtually a Liberal in all but name.) Rather, the mass of Midlanders sought to achieve their basic rights through their own organizations. Of these, trade unionism was the dominant movement.

The growth of unionism in the Midlands began with local craft and friendly societies in the early years of the nineteenth century and gathered momentum throughout Victoria's reign. Its strength varied widely, reflecting the variety of occupational and social conditions within the region. In the metal trades of the Birmingham/Black Country conurbation the small scale of workshop production largely prevented employees joining together, union activity being easily spotted and repressed by the employers. Only in the larger companies were groups such as the Amalgamated Society of Engineers able to make much headway. Attempts were made consistently throughout the era to bring together all unions under one umbrella organization. But by the last quarter of the nineteenth century a distinct split had occurred between skilled workers (such as silversmiths, masons, turners and cabinet-makers), who had served an apprenticeship and thus sought to safeguard their relatively well-paid jobs and social positions, and the mass of semi-skilled and unskilled workers. Self-interest promoted some strange decisions. In 1875 the Royal Commission on Factory and Workshop Acts proposed to raise the minimum age of full-time work from 13 years to 14 years of age. Birmingham officials of the National Society of Amalgamated Brassworkers bitterly opposed the suggestion because their craftsman members relied on cheap boy labour to compete with semi-skilled, cut-price competitors for work sub-contracted by the larger manufacturers.

Getting Away from It All

Travel for leisure purposes was largely unknown before the late nineteenth century. Annual functions such as Nottingham's Goose Fair or the Stratford Mop would attract visitors from neighbouring settlements, but these were exceptions. Before the growth of the railway network, journeys were slow and costly. Besides, even the largest pre-industrial towns had open fields and woodlands within easy reach. Massive urbanisation of the countryside, however, wiped out such areas. The beer-house and the brothel became the only centres of everyday amusement for millions of industrial urbanites.

40 Trade unions were treated with intense suspicion by governments and employers. Thus the membership card of the Amalgamated Society of Engineers shows a worker rejecting the sword offered by the soldier while his companion accepts the scroll of learning.

Some local authorities tried to provide alternative recreational facilities. Leicester's New Walk was developed as early as 1785 and the first purpose-built urban park (Derby Arboretum) was laid out in 1839. Birmingham was one of the first cities to open a public library (1861) and an art gallery (1867) Local working-class amusements, such as cock-fighting, rat-killing and badger-drawing, survived into the 1880s; so too did whippet-racing, especially in the Black Country. But these pastimes were gradually suppressed and replaced by organized team games. Professional football emerged in the 1870s with Aston Villa, who became league champions in 1897, dominating the Midlands' scene in the early years.

'Getting away from it all' on a large scale really began with the cheap excursion train. One such outing in 1840, from Nottingham to Leicester, 'had four engines to drag it forward, and to the beholder appeared like a moving street, the houses of which were filled with human beings . . . The number of carriages was 67, and the number of passengers nearly 3,000 . . .' Throughout the late Victorian period, more and more of the population gained paid holidays. However, apart from those areas close to the big urban centres which could be visited comfortably on bank holidays by train or tram, the countryside was still more or less undisturbed. Thousands of workers preferred to flock to the seaside each summer. The resorts chose their visitors carefully. Blackpool, Margate, Rhyl and Weston-Super-Mare became targets for working-class outings. Bournemouth, Torquay and Worthing, on the other hand, actively discouraged the day-tripper. The latter brought little money into the town and often scared away those who brought a great deal! Such resorts looked towards wealth and social status, their aim being to provide 'the amusements of which polite society is especially fond'.

41 The Promenade, Paignton (Devon), about 1898. Despite its distance, the seaside resort was a popular target for many middle-class Midland families.

6
The Legacy of Competition

The competitive spirit, upon which Victorian power and prosperity was based, eventually became an agent of destruction. Many small towns and rural communities, no longer able to sell their products in the face of urban competition, dwindled almost to the point of extinction. At Alton in north-east Staffordshire, for example, the manufacture of brass, begun by Thomas Patten in 1734, had ceased with the transfer of production to Oakamoor in 1828.

42 The old . . . women sewing lace at Shaldon in 1911.

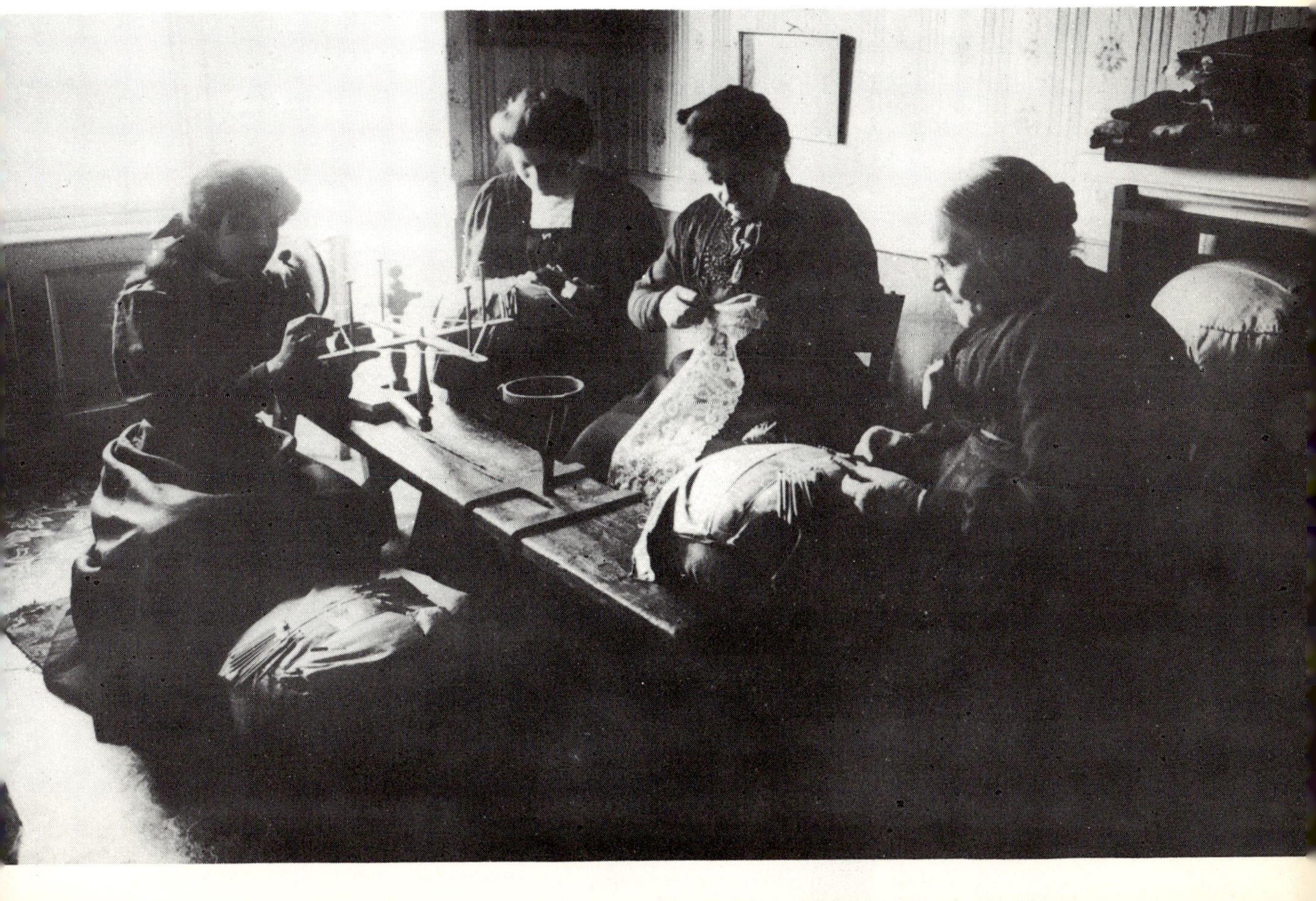

Alton Mill, having three waterwhells, was converted to paper production, but the business could not compete with Scandinavian imports and it collapsed shortly after the turn of the century throwing a few dozen people out of work. Again, the copper mines of Ecton in the Manifold valley, worked from at least as early as 1640, finally closed in 1889. The village was subsequently depopulated, but the visitor may still observe the engine-house and other remains which lie below the massive spoil-heap that covers the entrance to Dutchman Mine.

On a national scale, competition between the forces of capital and labour led to a series of clashes between employers and unions that culminated in the General Strike of 1926. The employers' victory ushered in a period of repression which saw the unions lose many of the rights for which they had fought so hard during the Victorian era. (Unionists distributing recruiting leaflets outside Austin Motors in Birmingham in the 1930s were regularly harassed by the police and frequently arrested for obstruction or causing a breach of the peace.) And at the international level, competition for the world's resources and markets led to the disastrous Great War (1914-18) and the industrial recession of the following two decades.

The years from the death of Victoria in 1901 to the outbreak of the Second World War (1939) were not entirely bleak and unrewarding. Tremendous advances were made in the provision of decent family homes, in standards of clothing and nutrition, in the variety of leisure activities available and in opportunities for higher education. But the problems of the inter-war period cast a long shadow over the lives of many Midland families. Alan Sillitoe, in his autobiographical novel *Key to the Door*, describes a free dinner centre in Nottingham in the 1930s: 'The breakfast, when it did come, was magnificent: three slices of bread and butter each, and a mug of milky cocoa. There was no breakfast to beat it, as far as Brian knew, except tomatoes and bacon, but that was a dinner.'

Epitaph for an Era

The 1901 Census gives a detailed picture of the changes that had occurred in the Midlands during the preceding century. In 1801, only 19 per cent of the people of England lived in towns of over 20,000 inhabitants; by 1901, this figure had risen to around 75 per cent. At the beginning of the nineteenth century the market towns of Shrewsbury, Worcester and Oxford were amongst the ten largest Midland settlements. By 1901 they had been overtaken in size by the greatly expanded industrial centres of Walsall, West Bromwich and Hanley (in the Potteries).

The later census reveals that growth in industrial towns and stagnation elsewhere was not consistent throughout the nineteenth century. In 1889 the Black Country's historian, F.W. Hackwood, was already lamenting the decline of the iron industry in the area: 'To stand on Church Hill [in Wednesbury] at night and gaze around on the busy scene of myriad fires belching forth like so many volcanoes was a sight not easily forgotten. But all this has passed away now . . .' Again, the textile mills of Belper, Cromford, Milford and Glossop all suffered from severe competition in the last quarter of the century and their misfortunes prompted local out-migration. Conversely, considerable expansion was recorded in many East Midland villages during the decade before 1901. The introduction of machinery into the hosiery trades of Nottingham and Leicester caused a decline in the domestic side of the industry which thrived in the outlying villages. Eventually, shortage of labour in the cities forced manufacturers into the countryside to utilize the work-force their machines had replaced. Thus new hosiery factories sprang up in settlements such as Wigston Magna, Hinckley, Market Harborough and Southwell.

The most spectacular growth in the latter part of the nineteenth century occurred on the outskirts of the major cities. Improvements in urban transport allowed for the rapid expansion of the built-up area. Birmingham in particular was 'swallowing up its immediate suburbs', with whole suburbs like Moseley and Handsworth in the course of being submerged in the urban flood. A contemporary Birmingham commentator wrote that 'these now old villages often present some curious anachronisms. A grey old church, partly buried by a

43 . . . and the new. This bizarre float appeared in the Lady Godiva Show at Coventry in 1897. The three-wheeled Motette is perched on a Cannstatt-Daimler commercial vehicle.

44 Girl and her grandmother, about 1914. The woman wears the heavy clothes typical of the Victorian era whereas the child is dressed in a light, loose-fitting costume popular in Edwardian times.

hoary fat churchyard, is surrounded by the most modern of shops and stores; and a primitive little bow-windowed cottage, with a few flower pots in the window, has perchance, a glaring ginship next door'. The rate of growth of such districts was often astonishing. Erdington in north Birmingham, for example, grew from a village of 2,599 people in 1881 to a major suburb of 16,368 in 1901. Here the tram was responsible for development. In Northfield, to the south of the city, which increased its population by over 100 per cent in the decade 1891-1901, the railway was the agent of colonization.

A 'Golden Age'

Although Edward VII was king for only nine years (1901-10), his reign is remembered as a 'golden age', a decade of gaiety between the restraints of Victorian society and the catastrophe of the First World War. But it was only the upper classes who could follow the extravagant, pleasure-loving pursuits of the new king. For the great majority of Midlanders, life continued in the Victorian pattern until 1914. The introduction of old-age pensions, labour exchanges and national insurance did a little to alleviate the condition of the poor, but desperate poverty remained a common feature of both urban and rural life in the Midlands. In fact, the gap between the rich and the poor grew larger during the Edwardian period. Moreover, it was no longer possible to speak of the 'working class' or the 'middle class' as it had been in the nineteenth century. These two broad groups contained a range of families with marked variations in their income and lifestyle.

Wage differentials within the ranks of the skilled workers in the Midlands were not particularly great during Edward's reign. A skilled Stoke potter received about £90 per year in 1906 while Birmingham jewellers averaged £97 and Coventry watchmakers about £94 per year. (The skilled boot and shoemakers of Rushden, Kettering and Wellingborough were relatively poorly paid, receiving an average yearly wage of only £71 in 1906.) Only coalface workers in Nottinghamshire (£112 a year), Stourbridge glassblowers (£113 a year) and railway engine drivers (£119 a year) earned wages substantially above the regional average for skilled men in 1906. There were marked differences, however, between the wages of the skilled and unskilled worker. For example, a pottery thrower earned around £93 in 1906 while a semi-skilled packer would only pick up £78 per year and an unskilled labourer around £56. Similarly, a labourer in an engineering factory in Coventry and Rugby averaged just £52 per year, whereas a machineman made £84 and a top mechanic around £106. Sharp differences also existed within the professional occupations. A qualified male teacher in 1913 earned around £155 per annum, a doctor about £395 and a solicitor around £560. (Women received roughly half the income of their male colleagues in all occupations. A nurse could earn £55 per year in 1913, a shorthand typist £62 but an experienced domestic servant only £46.)

45 The new age: advertising for a consumer society.

178 THE GRAPHIC August 8, 1891

Differences in income were naturally reflected in consumption patterns. A terraced 'tunnel-back' home sold for the relatively modest sum of £120 (such properites were usually rented at around 15 pence per week), whereas a five-bedroomed detached property fetched £600. A visitor to Worcester in 1903 could stay at the Star Hotel and part with 45 pence for a room and dinner, while an outlay of 22 pence would secure the same at the Victoria Temperance in Broad Street. Railway companies operated three-class trains – a first-class ticket from Stafford to Wolverhampton cost 14 pence in 1904, but a third class only 6½ pence. Two charges were made in municipal swimming baths, three pence for first class and 1½ pence for other bathers. Even beer had two prices – one pence per pint for 'rough ale' and 2½ pence for a smoother and less potent pint! Such social and economic divisions within society, however, barely survived the impact of the First World War.

'Pack Up Your Troubles'

The most telling effect of the Great War may be seen in hundreds of churches throughout the Midlands – the memorial tablet commemorating the young men who died in the mud-filled trenches of Flanders. On the first day of the Somme offensive, 76,000 soldiers died; 76,000 telegrams from the War Office devastated mean terraced houses and great country estates alike after just one day of fighting.

46 A wedding group, West Bromwich, about 1909. The family is well-dressed but there are indications that money is scarce – note the groom's ill-fitting 'off-the-peg' jacket and the everyday shoes worn by the girl sitting beside her father.

47 Home on leave. A soldier poses with his family before returning to the Belgian trenches.

48 Queuing for potatoes in Perry Barr, Birmingham, in 1916.

Two of the region's finest poets left contrasting statements on the war. Rupert Brooke of Rugby was a poet of national stature when he died of blood poisoning on the Greek island of Skyros during the ill-fated Gallipoli campaign. His poem *The Soldier*, which is inscribed on his memorial in Rugby School, evokes (as Winston Churchill wrote in an obituary in *The Times*) 'a willingness to die for the dear England whose beauty and majesty he knew. . [the] absolute conviction of the rightness of his country's cause'. Its opening lines:

If I should die, think only this of me:
That there's some corner of a foreign field
That is forever England. . .

struck a responsive chord in every wartime home. But those who returned from the fighting were unimpressed by Brooke's stirring patriotism. Rather it was Wilfred Owen, born in Oswestry but raised in Shrewsbury, who spoke for the common soldier. Although unrecognized as a poet before his death in Belgium in 1918, at the age of 25, Owen's poetry bears eloquent testimony to the horror of the 'war to end all wars':

Gas! Gas! Quick, boys! – An ecstasy of fumbling,
Fitting the clumsy helmets just in time;
But someone still was yelling out and stumbling
And flound'ring like a man in fire or lime . . .
Dim, through the misty panes and thick green light,
As under a green sea, I saw him drowning . . .

On the home front, the loss of so many young men brought a degree of emancipation to women. Some joined the Land Army and worked in the fields, others escaped from domestic service into shops, transport, industry and especially the munitions factories. In a short space of time, many girls were earning more in a week than they had previously earned in three months. But for the housewife, the war aggravated the problems of feeding a family. The submarine blockade cut Britain off from her overseas larders and although rationing was introduced it was by price, which naturally favoured the wealthy. Queuing for food became commonplace; many people joined queues without knowing exactly what they would be able to buy once they reached the counter.

With regard to local industry, the war often had a variable effect. A newspaper report of 1916 described the Birmingham Jewellery Quarter thus:

> You may go into workshop after workshop and see one side tenantless, idle, machinery still, tools lying on the bench. There is only one simile that leaps to the mind. It is that of a body paralysed down one side.

For those jewellery firms unable to secure government work, the war meant financial ruin. Yet other sectors of the industry expanded rapidly. In particular the medallists prospered, so too did the badgemakers and engravers. Similar beneficial effects were felt in the boot trade of Northamptonshire, amongst the Coventry ribbon-makers and in the saddlery workshops of Walsall. Even the Black Country ironmakers prospered – turning out shoes, nails and bits for army horses.

The Spread of Suburbia

Suburbanization was a product of new forms of transport. West Bridgford, across the River Trent to the south of Nottingham, numbered 280 people

49 Suburban transport: the motor bus in 1913.

and 58 houses in 1861. Following the rebuilding of the Trent Bridge in 1871, the village became popular as a dormitory suburb. The middle classes were carried into Nottingham at first by horse-drawn trams and, after 1901, by electric buses and trolley buses. By 1921, the town contained around 12,000 people. West Bridgford is typical of many such suburbs. It has uniform rows of terraces, all called roads, avenues, crescents or gardens, but never streets – the latter were associated with the problems of the central city. There is almost no industry and an absence of notable buildings. The strings of shops lie alongside one or two major roads.

Suburban sprawl was made possible not only by a cheap and flexible transportation network, but also by important changes in society. Successive Factory and Education Acts meant that after 1880 young children could not contribute to a family's income by working. Children, in other words, ceased to be units of production and became units of consumption. Large families were thus extremely costly to keep. If a middle-class family wanted to buy and furnish a suburban home and perhaps take an annual holiday at the seaside, they had to limit the size of their families. Hence the birth rate fell dramatically, from 30.8 births per 1,000 population in 1891 to 22.8 per 1,000 in 1921 and again to 15.8 in 1931. Sixty-one per cent of women married in England between 1870 and 1879 gave birth to five or more live children. For those marrying between 1900 and 1909, the figure fell to 28 per cent.

A second major social change concerned the role of women more directly. The rapid decline in the availability of servants forced a bigger domestic role upon the housewife. After 1920, the proliferation of both office jobs and light, clean, assembly work in modern factories provided young girls with alternative employment to domestic service. Moreover, the cost of employing a servant had to be weighed against the expense of a mortgage, the purchase of furniture and the cost of commuting. Technology responded to the housewife's need with a variety of innovations; vacuum cleaners, electric irons, gas and electric cookers and refrigerators were all available in the 1920s. Even more significant than these mechanical aids was the introduction of the radio, giving the housewife the daytime company she so badly needed.

50 A local authority built housing estate – Weoley Castle, Birmingham, 1939. Note the mock black and white frontage to the houses on the left, an attempt to break up the visual monotony of such estates.

Finally, the spread of the suburban Midlands is associated with changing attitudes towards the labouring classes by both national and local governments. Fearing massive disaffection by urban working populations, a variety of municipal reforms were inaugurated. The Housing and Town Planning Act of 1919 introduced government subsidies for local authorities building council houses. Hence, through the inter-war period, large suburban estates were added to the major cities. Yet such schemes only touched the tip of the iceberg. Birmingham built nearly 58,000 municipal houses in the inter-war years. But at the end of this period, nearly 38,000 back-to-back houses (two rooms up, two rooms down, communal lavatory and wash-house) and 100,000 tunnel-back houses (three up, three down, but often without bathroom or indoor lavatory) remained within the city.

No Hands Needed

By 1921, the post-war boom had spent itself. For the remainder of the inter-war years Britain was in the grip of industrial recession. Unemployment rose to 22.1 per cent of the working population in 1932, never falling below 10 per cent over the whole period. 'No Hands Needed' became a familiar notice outside many factories throughout the country.

Those regions with a high proportion of the nation's staple industries (like textiles, shipbuilding and heavy engineering) were badly hit by wartime disruptions, contracting export markets and the necessity to modernize early Victorian plant and machinery. The Midlands escaped the worst excesses of the recession because the region was home to certain expanding industries. For example, between 1923 and 1938 the number of workers in the British motor industry more than doubled. By far the largest proportion of this increase was concentrated in the Midland centres of Birmingham, Solihull, Coventry, Derby and Oxford. The automobile industry stimulated the growth of associated sectors, such as electrical engineering (led by the Birmingham firm of Lucas), plastic components, leather goods (giving the Walsall saddlers a new lease of life), fabricated steel and tyres (represented by Dunlop in Birmingham and Goodyear in Wolverhampton).

The relative prosperity of the Midlands did not prevent its active participation in the political events which characterized the inter-war period. The inevitable conflict which followed the inability of successive governments (indcluding the first Labour administration of 1924) to solve the nation's

51 Employment in the automobile industry helped the Midlands to weather the worst of the inter-war storms. Mass production techniques increased the demand for labour. This photograph shows the finishing shop of the Morris plant at Cowley, Oxford.

economic troubles led to the General Strike of 1926. Strictly speaking, the strike, called by the Trades Union Congress in support of the miners who were resisting wage cuts, was not 'general'. Many unions affiliated to the TUC were not instructed to take part. Nevertheless, there was an amazing response to the call for strike action by the railwaymen and other transport workers, engineers, electricians, iron and steel workers and newspaper employees. Birmingham awoke on 4 May to find no passenger transport and virtually no newspapers. Every one of the largest fleet of municipal buses in the world remained in its garage. That evening, Sutton Coldfield dimmed its street lighting to conserve power and hundreds of commuters groped their way homewards by bicycle or on foot. But in general, the fabric of normal life was relatively untouched. There were no gas or electricity cuts to bring the reality of the strike into the home, road transport (organized by the employers) proved capable of moving foodstuffs and effective police action enabled volunteers to man signal boxes, drive buses and work machinery. After nine days the TUC backed down. The miners fought on alone until August of 1926 when, beaten by the threat of starvation, they were forced to accept both cuts in wages and a longer working day.

The aftermath of the strike saw a dramatic fall in both trade union membership and industrial militancy. At a broad level, victimization of strikers by employers left a legacy of bitterness. Certain firms, such as Averys of West Bromwich and Tangyes of Smethwick, insisted that all strikers re-apply for their jobs – many were laid off. The Tramways Department of Birmingham Corporation and the Midland Red Company stated that in future they would refuse to negotiate with the local unions. And certain of the railway companies withdrew the free travel passes from those of their workers who had obeyed the strike call.

The Daily Round

The upsurge in the British economy did not occur until 1939, when the nation was again at war. Yet although the inter-war period was largely characterized by its political struggles and the industrial depression, it is also remembered for a host of events which had varying effects upon the people of the Midlands.

In 1926, for example, a seemingly insignificant event occurred in Erdington. The first traffic island outside London was constructed. By 1933, the traffic problem in Birmingham's city centre was so severe that a unique one-way system was introduced. Chaos reigned for several days until drivers became accustomed to the innovation. (The wheel has recently turned full circle – motorists are now banned from several roads in the central area.) For members of the Metropolitan Works Band of Saltley, 1925 was a milestone in their history. In that year the band won every contest it entered; in one day alone it took six firsts! But for Black Country dog fanciers, 1932 was a year to remember: Wild Woolley, a local dog, won the Greyhound Derby by one of the largest margins ever recorded. Sporting facilities in those years regularly attracted far more supporters than do modern events. Thousands flocked to county cricket matches to watch their favourites, not least of whom was George Gunn, who delighted Trent Bridge crowds in the late 1920s with the audacity of many of his strokes. His speciality was a shot behind his body, in between pads and wicket, to a ball on the leg side! Supporters of the Albion rejoiced in 1931 when the West Bromwich team, largely through the genius of Billy Richardson, crushed local rivals Birmingham City in the F.A. Cup Final, but lamented four years later when another Wembley appearance brought defeat.

Leisure patterns, though, were changing rapidly. The 1930s was the period when the mass media – press, radio, film – first began to assume their modern form. Most households owned a radio by the middle of the decade, but the BBC only offered, as the sociologist Noreen Branson remarked, 'traditional middle-class culture, self-improvement tempered by triviality, and establishment views'. The network did bow to ordinary tastes, however, with a series of gardening talks. (The new housing estates provided the first patch of garden for numerous families and the programme's presenter, Mr Middleton, was one of the earliest broadcasters to have a personal following of millions.) By 1937, it was estimated that 40 per cent of the British population attended the cinema at least once a week. For a relatively small cost, families could sit in the new, warm, plush suburban cinemas and watch two main feature films, a newsreel and a cartoon. Hollywood dominated the British screen and American films set the fashion in hairstyles, clothes and Christian names – Shirley (Temple), Marlene (Dietrich) and Gary (Cooper) were quickly adopted by Midland parents for their offspring.

The popularity of cinemas and dance-halls (as well as increases in the tax on beer) caused a decline in drinking as a leisure pastime. The big breweries hit back by building large suburban inns that incorporated smart lounges, for those who fought shy of the common bar, and party rooms for occasional dances and other functions. Mitchell and Butler, the brewers, aiming to re-create the homely atmosphere of the country pub but on a larger scale, ringed Birmingham with their monstrosities – mammoth mock Tudor, vast thatched cottage, huge Dutch colonial.

52 Will Morris' Celebrated Pierrots and Pierrettes, who performed in Birmingham parks and music-halls in the first quarter of the present century.

53 The growth of retail companies helped to widen the choice of commodities available to the housewife. This 1926 photograph shows one of the first George Mason (now International) stores in Birmingham.

Changing tastes and new materials had an effect upon other aspects of daily life. Although macintoshes were still made of rubber and knitted goods of real wool, the appearance in the 1930s of man-made fibres such as rayon heralded a new era of mass-produced, well-designed, cheap clothes. More and more branches of Woolworths were being opened, where nothing out of a wide range of household articles cost more than 2½ pence. Eating habits were also changing. For the unemployed and low-paid workers the regular diet still consisted of bread, margarine and tea, with a main meal of potatoes and cabbage with a little stewed meat for flavour. Fresh milk was relatively expensive, thus the tinned, condensed variety was preferred. For those families with a regular income, the rise of big food combines like Unilever's, Marsh and Baxter and Tate and Lyle, plus the introduction of pre-packaged convenience products such as blancmange powders, Quick Quaker oats and Ovaltine, meant that a fairly nutritious meal could be provided at a reasonable cost. The technique of canning brought a greater variety of food into the shops. Baked beans, tinned peas and tinned fruit became an important means of varying the diet in working-class homes. John Betjeman, the present Poet Laureate, recorded with distaste the gastronomic uniformity of the period:

Come, bombs, and blow to smithereens
Those air-conditioned bright canteens,
Tinned fruit, tinned meat, tinned milk, tinned beans,
Tinned minds, tinned breath.

7
The Midlands Today

The essential difference between the Great War and the 1939-45 conflict was the extension of the battlefield into the homes, farms and factories of the warring nations. Official figures put British civilian deaths at 60,000, a relatively small figure considering the massive destruction of property by enemy action.

54 A survivor of an air attack in 1941 surrounded by the debris of his bombed home.

Although the German airforce concentrated its attacks on the large industrial centres, people living in small towns and villages were not immune. Communities in the East Midlands in particular lived in fear of the bomb dropped at random by an aircraft lightening its load before flying home. No amount of elaborate precautions could prevent such an occurrence.

Within the cities, civil defence relied upon searchlights picking out bombers in the night sky and warnings being telephoned ahead. Air-raid sirens would sound in settlements below the flight-path of the aircraft and the population would scurry to its appointed shelters. Anti-aircraft guns located in parks and on wasteland generally had a poor record of actually shooting down the enemy, but their action undoubtedly reassured the local inhabitants. Inevitably, the greatest number of casualties were amongst those who inhabited the densely-peopled inner-city areas adjacent to the major industrial targets. In the early months of the war, children living in such districts were evacuated to rural areas. Wealthier citizens were also often able to remove themselves to the countryside, where there was both more food and greater personal security.

During the years following the Second World War the nation began to get to grips with the problems that had plagued the country during the inter-war years. The apparatus of a national health service was set up, the coal, railway and power companies were brought under state ownership and full employment was achieved for the first time in living memory. But there were immense difficulties to overcome, not least being the replanning and rebuilding of devastated central city areas. In an effort to improve Britain's trading position, sterling was devalued and the country entered a period of restraint on domestic spending. Above all, there was an appalling shortage of a host of articles, from tyres to saucepans, from oranges to hairpins.

Yet by the early 1950s it appeared that a corner had been turned. For the nation in general and the Midlands in particular this was marked by expansionist economic policies. For the individual family it was marked by the ending of food rationing. With the accession to the throne of a young Queen it seemed that a new age had dawned. Indeed, the minor news stories of 1952 and 1953 had a distinctly modern flavour. For example, Jack Jones (then Coventry district secretary of the Confederation of Shipbuilding and Engineering Unions) warned that 'We are going to have . . . the biggest fight we have had for years to maintain employment in the motor industry; competition is intense, particularly on the continent . . .' But the Midlands' motor trade was not alarmed. Although the budget of March 1952 increased the price of petrol to 21 pence per gallon and road tax from £2.50 to £12.50, cars were in great demand, so much so that new vehicles were restricted to people who had not previously purchased a post-war model. In October the new Queen opened the giant Claerwen Dam in mid-Wales which was intended to solve Birmingham's water problems 'for at least a century'. The year 1953 brought a major stoppage of work at Longbridge, an increase in the rate of interest on mortgages to 2½ per cent, a budget which Chancellor R.A. Butler declared to be 'tough enough to stem inflation', and a humiliating soccer defeat of England by the Hungarians at Wembley.

The Urban Network

The influence of a town or city reaches beyond its administrative boundary and the edge of its built-up area. The modern Midlands may be divided into the fields of influence of a few major urban areas, which offer a wide range of goods and services over a large area. These influence fields may be sub-divided into the catchment areas of smaller settlements, which provide a more restricted group of functions. (Some communities assume an importance far beyond that indicated by their size. On Ascension Day, Tissington, in the Derbyshire Peak District, receives coachloads of visitors eager to see the local wells bedecked with flowers. The Shrovetide football game at nearby Ashbourne similarly pulls in the crowds each year. Eastwood, a Nottinghamshire mining community with a population of just over 10,000, regularly attracts people from all over the world because of its association with the novelist D.H. Lawrence. And thousands flock to Stratford-upon-Avon each year to visit the memorials to William Shakespeare.)

Commuting, or the journey to work, is one of the clearest signs of a city's influence over its surrounding area. Before the Second World War, only those

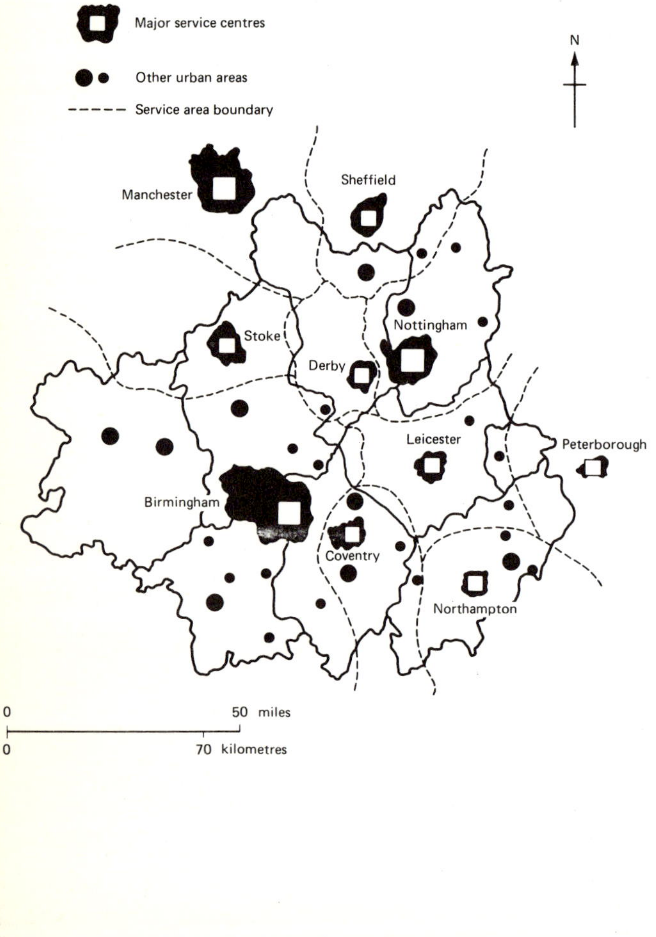

55 *left* The influence fields of the major Midland service centres.

56 *below* The growth of Oadby, 1950-1970.

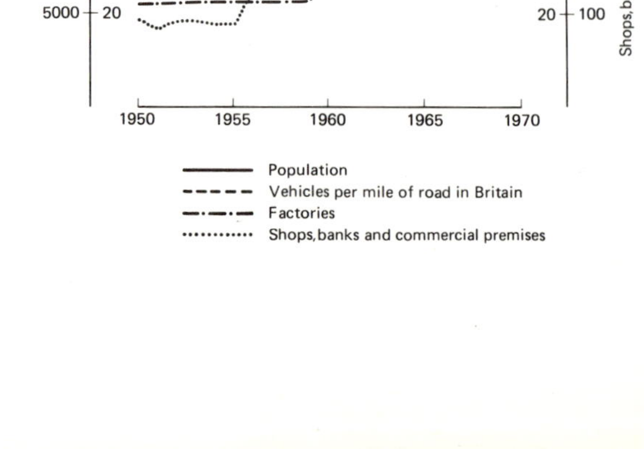

towns and villages which lay alongside the railway could export their working population into the local city each day. Outward expansion of the conurbations and other big urban centres had to await the massive rise in the private ownership of motor vehicles which took place after 1950. The motor car has enabled thousands of people to leave the large cities, settle in the small towns and villages scattered throughout the outlying region, and commute each day into the central city. Many of these settlements, hardly changed for hundreds of years, suddenly experienced a huge influx of population which completely altered their character.

Oadby, about six kilometres (four miles) to the south-east of Leicester, dates from the year 550. It remained a small agricultural community, apart from a local hosiery cottage industry, until the 1950s, unaffected by the growth of its large neighbour. Over the past 25 years Oadby's population has trebled, a period of expansion corresponding to the increase in private car ownership.

Oadby illustrates another common feature of outlying towns. At first, nearly all daily commuting trips were made into the central cities. But increasing dissatisfaction with rush-hour travelling has prompted people to seek local employment. Towns like Oadby therefore (Bromsgrove, Tamworth, Cannock, Solihull) have proved attractive to many small firms who are looking for new sites — and a willing labour force — for their operations. As such settlements develop they attract more and bigger services — retail, commercial, recreational — which in turn attract more people, and so on. The result is a complex urban network of large cities and small towns inter-linked through the movement of people, products and information.

Living

A visitor to the growth towns of Lichfield, Rugeley and Redditch, the modern shopping centres of Solihull and Wolverhampton, the redeveloped central areas of Coventry and Birmingham, the mechanized collieries of Nottinghamshire or the National Exhibition Centre may be excused for thinking that the Midlands has solved its more pressing problems. Relative to other areas in Britain, the Midlands of today is indeed a prosperous region. Yet despite its outward appearance, the region is still faced by an array of difficulties. Not least of these is the provision of decent family homes.

Thousands of nineteenth-century homes are still occupied throughout the Midlands, particularly in the cities. Many of these are without a bathroom, inside lavatory, proper ventilation or storage space. Through the 1950s and 1960s many local authorities carried out ambitious schemes for clearing slum areas and rehousing their populations. The table on page 87 shows why a population cannot be replaced in its entirety on the redeveloped site. Even with high-rise dwellings, present housing densities are much lower than those of a century ago. Besides, modern schools, shops, community centres and recreation facilities demand far more space than was allocated during the Victorian era.

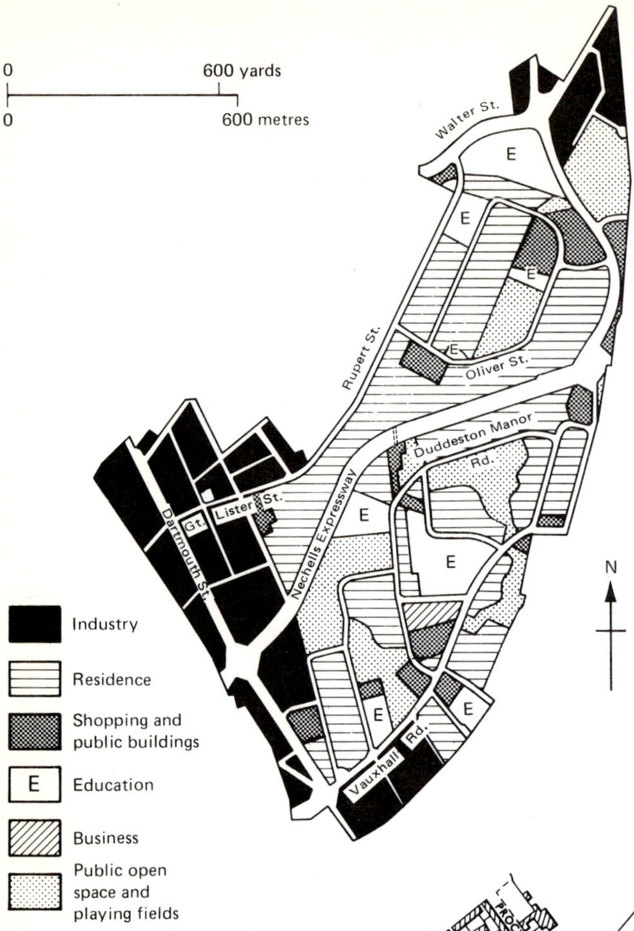

57 *below* Nechells comprehensive development area in 1950

58 *left* Nechells in 1972.

Population and land use in Birmingham's Comprehensive Development Areas						
District		Nechells	Newtown	Ladywood	Lee Bank	Highgate
Population	1952	19,062	28,125	24,418	14,797	16,484
	1972	12,537	15,400	12,448	6,531	10,080
Dwellings (number)	1952	5,885	9,349	7,558	4,492	4,886
	1972	3,635	4,467	3,609	1,894	2,924
Education (acres)	1952	8.0	12.9	4.6	3.4	6.0
	1972	27.0	39.9	25.3	12.7	32.1
Industry (acres)	1952	63.3	118.5	61.6	44.2	53.4
	1972	62.4	118.7	62.1	39.7	50.3
Open Space (acres)	1952	3.9	6.4	1.9	0.2	9.7
	1972	41.7	60.4	49.8	24.7	39.0

The two maps of the Nechells CDA illustrate the nature of inner area redevelopment. In 1950, the district was comprised of narrow streets of tightly packed houses, factories and tiny parcels of open space. After treatment, however, Nechells shows quite a different face. Schools enjoy large playgrounds, shops are grouped together away from the major through road, industry is restricted to a fringe zone and there is a generous acreage of public open space.

Inner area redevelopment in Birmingham between 1952 and 1972 meant that nearly 50,000 people (equivalent to the population of Kidderminster or Loughborough) had to be rehoused outside the CDAs. Traditionally, cities have relocated their displaced populations in housing estates built on vacant peripheral land within their boundaries. But as the years have passed, the availability of such land has diminished. One solution to this problem has been to export the surplus, or overspill, population to other urban areas.

Dozens of overspill schemes are now underway throughout the Midlands. Most of them involve moving fairly small numbers of people from the West Midland conurbation into the surrounding towns. Thus Lichfield has provided 1,200 houses for families from Walsall and Birmingham while Droitwich will develop, by 1986, seven residential areas together containing over 5,000 new homes for Birmingham emigrants. Certain of these programmes are being conducted on a far greater scale. Staveley is scheduled to receive over 40,000 people by the year 2000, Daventry will see its population rise from 12,000 in 1970 to 36,000 in 1981 and Wellingborough will have imported over 60,000 Londoners by 1981.

Even more significant in this context has been the designation of 'new towns'. These are designed not simply to absorb overspill populations but are intended to be effective growth centres which will counteract the influence of the major urban centres. Of the five Midland new towns, only Corby in Northamptonshire can claim to be an entirely new creation. Telford is a collection of towns and villages scatterd over the Shropshire Coalfield, Redditch is an old industrial centre closely linked to the Birmingham area and Peterborough and Northampton were important regional centres before being given new town status. Nevertheless, the provision in these settlements of new houses, industrial sites and modern shopping centres has given many Midland families the chance of shaping their lives in a different environment.

Wholesale slum clearance programmes appear to be a thing of the past. With the escalating cost of land and building materials, local authorities are now concentrating on improving sound homes in inner city and middle ring areas, so maintaining the complex social networks that have grown up over generations. Urban renewal schemes are not solely concerned with housing; they also concentrate upon the provision of jobs, community centres, shopping facilities and leisure activities.

Working

Modern employment patterns within the Midlands bear a close resemblance to those existing in the early part of this century. The manufacture of motor vehicles remains firmly rooted in the Birmingham-Coventry area, pottery production continues around Stoke and Northamptonshire still specializes in footwear. Around half of the national total employment in the knitwear industry is located in a zone stretching from Mansfield to Hinckley via Nottingham and Leicester, while most of the country's small metal goods are still

59 The scale of modern production: the industrial complex operated by British Celanese at Spondon, near Derby. Activities at this site include the production of man-made fibres, chemicals, plastics and steel tyre cord.

produced in the Black Country. Long Eaton continues to make lace and Leek to manufacture silk. Crystal glass still comes from Stourbridge and beer is still being brewed at Burton.

Despite this continuity of production, there have been considerable changes in the nature of employment since the 1950s. The most significant of these concerns the rise of the service industries like banking, retailing, transportation, administration and tourism. The service sector now employs around 51 per cent of the region's workforce, compared to some 38 per cent in 1951. The corresponding decrease in numbers employed in the manufacturing sector has meant that industrial concerns have had to either mechanize production or increase the productivity of their labour force. For many firms, the competition for workers from the service industries resulted in a continued shortage of labour through the 1950s and 1960s. This problem was only partially solved by the immigration of people from other parts of Britain and from overseas.

Important changes have also taken place within the manufacturing and extractive sectors. Coal-mining, for example, has seen a reduction in both output and employment over the past 20 years. Only one colliery (Granville) works the Shropshire Coalfield, eight survive in north Staffordshire but the last of the south Staffordshire mines closed in the mid-1960s. In the East Midlands the collieries exploiting the exposed coalfields in Derbyshire are gradually becoming worked out or too expensive to mine because of the broken nature of the coal seams. In 1957 there were 25 collieries employing about 27,000 men in the Erewash valley. By 1969 only 13,000 miners remained working the 11 surviving collieries. By contrast, mining has recently expanded on to the concealed coalfield in Nottinghamshire prompting the opening of large pits like Bevercotes, Cotgrave and Calverton. A similar pattern of development has characterized the steel industry. Iron-making has virtually disappeared from the Black Country. In its other traditional location, the Alfreton-Ripley area of Derbyshire, it is represented only by the Stanton Iron Works near Ilkeston. Steel is still made at Brierley Hill and Wednesbury as well as at Bilston. Plants such as Round Oak, relying mainly on steel scrap for their raw materials, continue in production largely because of the local West Midland steel-consuming market. Expansion in Midland steel-making has only occurred in recent years in the Corby area of Northamptonshire where a large British Steel plant exploits local iron-ore deposits.

Both coal-mining and steel-making have been influenced by national government policies. So too has the motor vehicles industry. Anxious to aid those regions with high unemployment rates and low rates of industrial investment, successive governments have directed growth in the vehicles sector to Scotland, South Wales, Merseyside and the North-East. Nevertheless, over 200,000 people in the West Midlands are currently involved in the vehicles industry. Apart from government intervention in determining the location of new plants, the major characteristic of the vehicles industry since 1950 has been the growth of four giant firms – the state-owned British Leyland and the American concerns of Ford, Chrysler and General Motors. A few small, independent manufacturers like Morgan at Malvern and Reliant of Tamworth still service a specialized market, but the closure of Jensen of West Bromwich in the mid-1970s indicates the difficulties facing such companies.

Grave problems have also been experienced by the motorcycle manufacturers. Foreign, particularly Japanese, competition has hit domestic firms hard. Inputs of government money, plus a pruning of the labour force, failed to save the Birmingham firm of BSA, while the Triumph factory at Meriden struggles on as a workers' co-operative. Textile imports have similarly hit the clothing producers of the East Midlands. The English Sewing Cotton Company's factory at Belper is one of the last remaining cotton mills in the Midlands.

The continued prosperity of the industrial Midlands may no longer be automatically assumed. Within the western part of the region a too heavy dependence upon the vehicles sector may prove a disadvantage. Similar problems resulting from specialization may ultimately affect the textile areas in the east. Diversification of production, particularly into the growth sectors of electronics, domestic electrical engineering and petrochemicals, has proceeded relatively slowly within the region. In the mid-1970s only the Erewash valley qualified for certain types of government benefits for firms locating in that area. Over the next 30 years, other problem districts may be forced to seek such aid in an attempt to attract employment into their locality.

The Changing Countryside

Since 1950, the demands of urban areas, transportation systems, industrial activities and recreation facilities for rural land have brought changes to the Midland countryside as great in magnitude as were the effects of enclosure movements in the eighteenth century.

Farming, too, has been responsible for dramatic alterations in the landscape. Large-scale mechanical production of cereals and vegetables, often by massive food corporations like Libbys, Birds Eye, Rank-Hovis-McDougall and Nabisco, has caused a huge increase in field size by the removal of hedges. (In 1975 alone, it is estimated that over 643 kilometres (400 miles) of hedgerow were removed in Warwickshire.) The dangers of destroying such field systems were made clear in the early 1970s when high winds, unimpeded by hedges, stripped the topsoil from thousands of hectares of farmland in the eastern borders of the region. Other modern innovations include battery techniques where animals, particularly poultry, are raised in factory-type units, new crops like soy-bean and maize and 'pick-your-own' products, in which farmers cut their labour and transport costs by inviting urbanites to harvest their own fruit and vegetables.

60 *right* Holme Pierrepont, Nottinghamshire. A national water-sports centre is being created on the site of old gravel pits.

61 *left* Bottle ovens in the Potteries around 1906. The Pottery Industry Preservation Trust has saved some kilns such as these and is creating a working museum in the existing buildings at Gladstone Pottery, Longton.

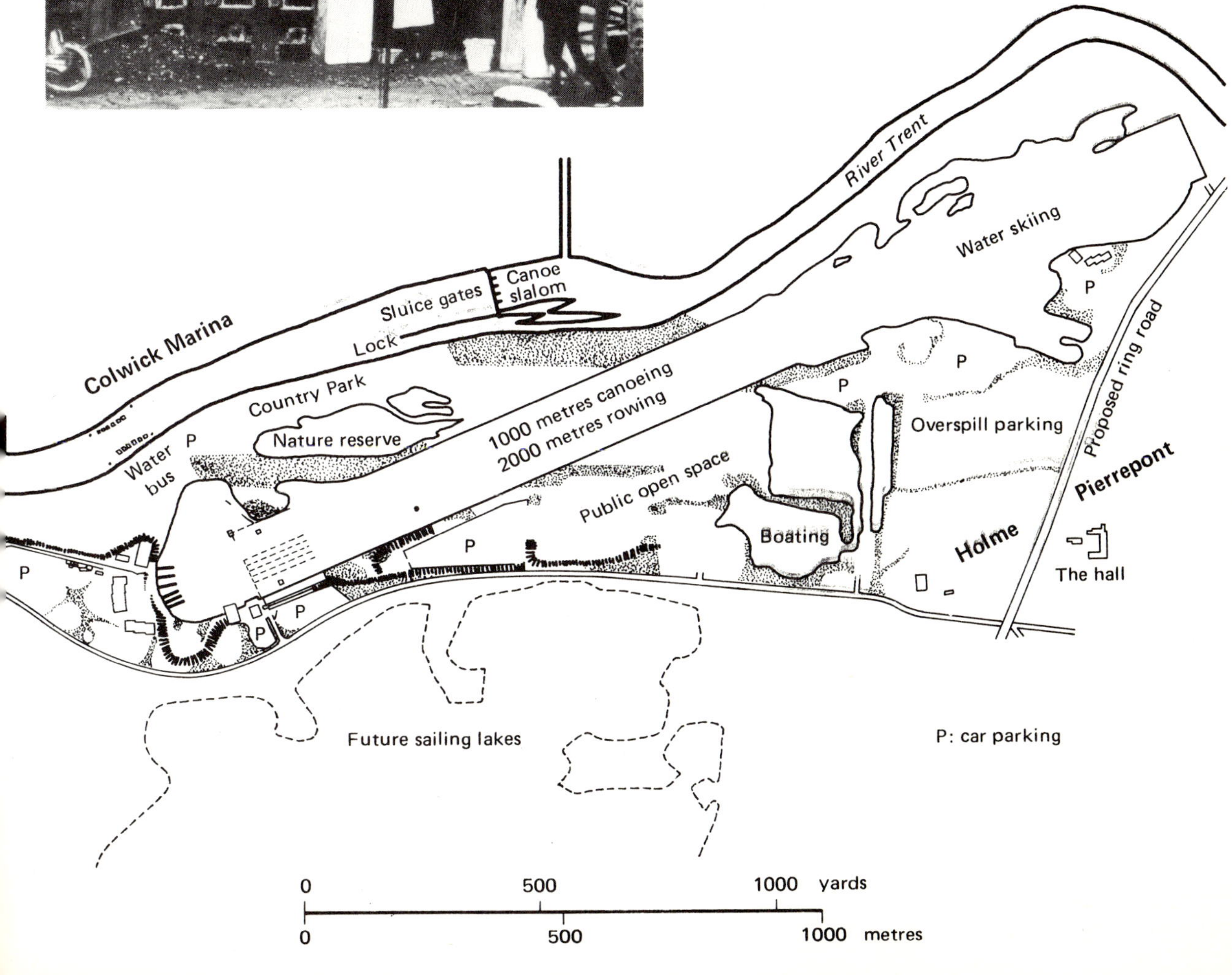

As each year passes, the land area given over to agricultural pursuits declines. Urban expansion is the greatest consumer of rural land in the Midlands. Space is needed not just for low-density housing, shopping facilities and commercial and industrial functions, but also for schools and playing fields, sewage plants, health centres and road networks. Each mile of motorway constructed, for example, requires 11 hectares (27 acres) of land!

Urban expansion on such a scale has been made possible through the rapid rise in the private ownership of motor vehicles. The same factor has been responsible for the growth in rural leisure activities. Bewdley Safari Park, Elvaston Country Park outside Derby and the conversion of part of the Shropshire Union Canal at Newport into an amenity area for boating and fishing all attract the city dweller. So do rural zoos like Twycross in Leicestershire, transportation activities such as the Severn Valley Railway and the Crich Tramway Museum in Derbyshire (which attracts over 100,000 visitors each year), the opening of stately homes like Alton Towers in Staffordshire and the creation of water sports centres such as the Cotswold Water Park in the upper Thames valley. Activites such as these may generate a wide range of problems. In the Peak District National Park, for example, upwards of 50,000 visitors can be expected on a fine Sunday in summer. Such a large number could be easily accommodated throughout the Park, but the majority of visitors congregate in relatively small areas like the Goyt valley and Dovedale. Cars may be banished to large car-parks, but this does not prevent soil erosion caused by the tramping of thousands of pairs of feet. Only the constant re-routing of footpaths and the creation of no-go zones can prevent the visitor from destroying the landscape he has come to enjoy.

A Future from the Past

It is doubtful whether many inhabitants of the Midlands consider themselves to be 'Midlanders'. The region lacks the physical uniformity of the South-West of England, the industrial unity of the North-East or the political identity of Wales. The people of Herefordshire and western Shropshire derive their lilting speech and many of their agricultural practices from Wales; the inhabitants of Buxton, Glossop and Macclesfield turn to Manchester for shopping and entertainment while the people of the eastern Cotswolds often commute into the towns of the Thames Basin. Again, the expertise in metal-working common to the West Midlands is largely absent from the East, whereas the knowledge of textile production enjoyed by the inhabitants of Leicester and Nottingham is relatively unknown in Birmingham and Wolverhampton. And only Stoke-on-Trent is a centre of skill in the manufacture of pottery and china.

Yet despite these, and many other, intra-regional differences, the Midlands does have a certain uniformity. Nowhere else in Britain may the complete historical record of the nation be seen so clearly written on the landscape. And perhaps nowhere else is there so great a danger of that record being obliterated in the coming years.

A traveller may pass in a day from the bleak windswept moorlands of Shropshire with their ancient trackways and hill forts, via the Roman town of Leintwardine, along lanes and through villages laid down in Saxon times to the Norman walls of Ludlow Castle and the planned Medieval town beyond. Eastwards the road passes through Tenbury Wells (which enjoyed a brief moment of glory in the early nineteenth century as a spa town) before dropping down to the Severn at the Medieval river port of Bewdley. Further on the traveller will pass through the early industrial communities of Halesowen, Rowley Regis and Dudley, where the traditional Black Country dialect (with a grammatical structure similar to that used by early Saxon immigrants) may be heard, alongside the language of more recent immigrants from India and Pakistan. After a few miles the rebuilt city centre of Birmingham is encountered, characterized by its ugly concrete and glass office blocks and a hugely expensive inner ring road that cuts the city centre off from its outer area like the walls of some Medieval town.

Swinging north-eastwards, the traveller will cross both Watling Street (now the A5) and the M1 motorway before reaching Braunstone on the outskirts of Leicester, where the headquarters of the British Shoe Corporation denotes Leicester's position as the premier boot and shoe producer in the region. Beyond the suburban fringes at Thurmaston and Syston the road enters a district colonized not by Saxons but by Danes. (The 'by' ending of Dalby, Somerby and Rearsby betrays their origin as Danish settlements.) Northwards another Roman road, the Fosse Way, skirts the Vale of Belvoir which lies to the south. (The Vale is now threatened by the plans of the National Coal Board to extract millions of tons of coal from beneath its fertile soils.) Past Newark, the royalist stronghold in the Civil War, the traveller may follow the River Trent on its northern journey as it winds through a low-lying countryside drained with the help of Dutch engineers in the Middle Ages, now given over to large-scale cereal production and dotted with gigantic power stations. Finally, in the farthest corner of Nottinghamshire, the junction of the Chesterfield Canal with the River Trent at West Stockwith serves as a reminder of an industrial presence a few dozen kilometres to the west around the old iron-making centres of Eckington, Staveley and Dronfield.

In future years our descendants may view our present achievements not so much in terms of how many kilometres of motorway were built and vehicles produced, or in terms of office blocks constructed and supermarkets opened, or even in terms of tons of coal mined or units of electricity generated. Rather we may be judged in terms of how carefully we conserved our urban heritage and the monuments to our industrial history, and how well we preserved the character of our landscape. And, above all, how successful we were in providing equal opportunities for all Midlanders to share in the richness and diversity of their environment.

Further Reading

Baker, A.R.H. and Harley, J.B., *Man Made the Land,* David and Charles, 1973
Burke, G., *Towns in the Making,* Arnold, 1971
Chambers, J.D. and Chapman, S.D., *The Beginnings of Industrial Britain,* University Tutorial Press, 1970
Cherry, G., *Urban Change and Planning,* Foulis, 1972
Hoskins, W.G., *The Making of the English Landscape,* Hodder and Stoughton, 1955
Hoskins, W.G., *English Landscapes,* BBC Publications, 1973
Lofts, N., *Domestic Life in England,* Weidenfeld and Nicholson, 1976
Newbold, E.B., *Warwickshire History Makers,* EP Publishing, 1975
Reader, W.J., *Victorian England,* Batsford, 1964
Robinson, A. and Millward, R., *The West Midlands,* Macmillan, 1971
Robinson, A. and Millward, R., *The Welsh Marches,* Macmillan, 1970
Rogers, A., *This Was Their World; Approaches to Local History,* BBC Publications, 1972
Rowley, T., *The Shropshire Landscape,* Hodder and Stoughton, 1972
Smith, D.M., *The Industrial Archaeology of the East Midlands,* David and Charles, 1965
Steane, J., *The Northamptonshire Landscape,* Hodder and Stoughton, 1973
Wise, M.J. (ed.), *Birmingham and its Regional Setting,* British Association for the Advancement of Science, 1950
Whybrow, J. (ed.), *How Does Your Birmingham Grow?,* Whybrow, 1972

Index

The numbers in **bold** type are the figure numbers of the illustrations